THE CHURCH AS SALT

Is the church dying? In this profound and joyful book, Sally Douglas argues that we are not living through a period of decline but of great opportunity. The church is called to be 'salt' – not to succeed, not to triumph over the world, but to bring out the best in the world just as salt seasons a meal. With colourful stories from church history and from the present, Douglas illustrates the numerous functions of salt, and shows how congregations today can be 'seasoning pockets of grace' for the sake of the world. This is a generous, encouraging, challenging account of the difference Christian discipleship makes.

Ben Myers
Associate Professor
Alphacrucis College

'The church is dying... Thanks be to God.' So writes theologian and pastor, Sally Douglas, on the opening page of this engaging and accessible book. The church as a custodian of morals, a purveyor of respectability, a friend of empire, is all coming to an end. It is now time to tell a 'different story'. To break free from this dying church, Sally richly employs Jesus' image of his disciples being salt – an inconspicuous but transforming agent – to help us re-think and re-make our church communities as salty communities. Vigorously resisting the abiding and tempting narratives of success, numbers, power and nostalgia, Sally invites us to engage a variety of life-giving visions of the church. Whilst the book is rich with deep theological insights, it is not abstract. She provides us with snapshots of actual, living, breathing Christian communities scattered across the Uniting Church. Each in its own way has been discovering ways of reflecting the way of Jesus in their worship and mission. Incorporating questions for discussion and suggestions for prayer, the book is an ideal resource for church communities or individual members who want to hear this 'different story' about the past and the future of the church. Such readers will be challenged. But they will not be disappointed.

Geoff Thompson
Associate Professor of Systematic Theology
Pilgrim Theological College, University of Divinity

While small in size, the book is big on wisdom, passion and insight. Using the metaphor of salt for the community of the church and the discipleship of Jesus followers, Sally takes her readers on a journey to rediscover how to live as a salty church, on the edge, passionate about flavouring the world with God's good news. Drawing on Scripture, early Christian writers and stories from contemporary salty churches and people, readers are invited into the hard, vulnerable, joyous, justice-seeking life of salty Jesus followers. Beautifully written with clear, poetic language and exquisite images, this book both draws its readers into prayerful reflection and provokes into active salty living. I recommend this book for anyone intrigued by Jesus and wondering what his life might mean for you and the world and for those seeking to live more faithfully to Jesus' way. I even more recommend you find a group to read and reflect with. The wondering questions, a simply reflective activity, a prayer at the end of each chapter and Pearl Taylor's accompanying images allow each reader to ponder deeply the implications of being salt and living salty.

Sharon Hollis
President
Uniting Church in Australia

In *The Church As Salt*, Sally Douglas offers a metaphor that is at once a relief and at the same time a reminder. Critiquing addictions to congregational numbers, corporate plans, and metrics of significance, she reminds her readers of the simplicity — and demand — of following a gospel that is seen more in generosity, neighbourliness, gathering, vulnerability and sharing than in the competitive and exhausting culture that religion sometimes occupies. She knows that leadership in a church can be lonely, and knows, too, that participation in a congregation doesn't suit everyone. Instead she points to organic ways of meeting, where the local needs are considered, and where comparison is placed where it should be: outside. In her easy — and studied — prose, we meet church leaders, church congregants, church matriarchs and patriarchs and biblical characters, all presented with a love for their lives and for the ways they tried to live with authenticity in the circumstances that faced them. For Sally Douglas, a Christian witness can be small, granular, mourning, growing, unseen, continuing and nurturing. It doesn't need to be exhausting, humiliating, corporate or dominant. In scholarship, story and vision, *The Church As Salt* is a compelling read and — more — a call to the local.

Pádraig Ó Tuama
Poet and Theologian
Host of *Poetry Unbound*

THE CHURCH ~~TRIUMPHANT~~ AS SALT

Becoming the Community Jesus Speaks About

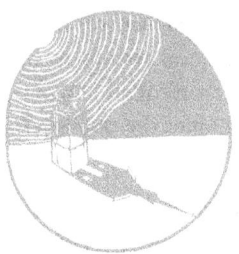

— SALLY DOUGLAS —

COVENTRY PRESS

Published in Australia by
Coventry Press
33 Scoresby Road
Bayswater VIC 3153

ISBN 9780648982265

Copyright © Sally Douglas 2021

All rights reserved. Other than for the purposes and subject to the conditions prescribed under the *Copyright Act*, no part of this publication may be reproduced, stored in a retrieval system, or transmitted in any form or by any means, electronic, mechanical, photocopying, recording or otherwise, without the prior permission of the publisher.

Scripture quotations are from the *New Revised Standard Version Bible* © 1989, Division of Christian Education of the National Council of the Churches of Christ in the United States of America. Used by permission. All rights reserved.

Catalogue-in-Publication entry is available from the
National Library of Australia http://catalogue.nla.gov.au

Cover design by Ian James – www.jgd.com.au
Text design by Coventry Press
Illustrations by Pearl Taylor – Paperpearl.com.au
Typeset in Fontin 11 pt

Printed in Australia

Table of Contents

Acknowledgments	9
Chapter One	
The church as salt	11
Chapter Two	
The littleness of salt	21
Chapter Three	
Salty tears	45
Chapter Four	
Dark salty wombs	65
Chapter Five	
Salt that preserves	93
Chapter Six	
Salt as seasoning	117
Chapter Seven	
Sweaty conclusions	141

Acknowledgments

Andrew, my beloved co-conspirator, your enthusiasm for this book and your critical eye have been gifts in the writing. Ian David, Sandy, Natalie, Salesi and Rachel, thank you for trusting me with your stories.

I also extend my thanks and love to the people of Richmond Uniting and to all the early church writers I continue to dialogue with. Kylie M, dear friend, I am grateful that, standing on the beach together, you gave voice to my tucked away wondering about art for the book. Pearl, thank you for saying yes! Your deep and prayerful engagement with each chapter has brought forth breathtaking artwork. I am astonished.

Hugh from Coventry, thank you for encouraging me to begin this book in the first place. It has been a joy to write.

This book was mostly written in the midst of parish life in extended lockdown. I am grateful for all the cheesy toast (salt sprinkled) lunch breaks with the crew during this strange time. Jemimah and Zach, we love you so much.

My prayer is that this book will challenge and nourish in equal measure and that it may be a companion for the journey if you are reading alone or in community.

In the name of Christ, the delicious, disruptive bread of life.

Sally

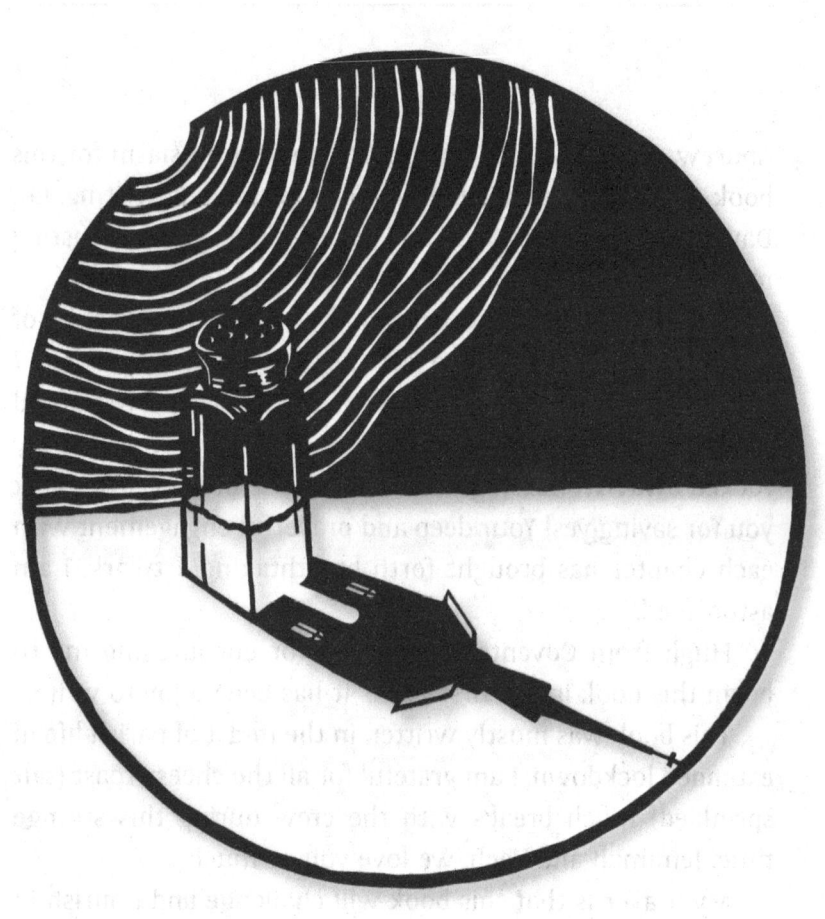

Chapter One

The church as salt

'The church is dying' is recited like a mantra and presented as a fact in congregations, church meetings and in media articles. When we say something often enough, we tend to believe it. However, I remain unconvinced by the hype about church decline. I think something far more interesting – and more costly – is occurring in the West. The church as a social club is dying. The church as signifier of cultural respect is dying. The church as the authoritative 'purity police' is dying. Thanks be to God. The church is not dying, but the church is being refined. We are being called to face our self-deceptions and our collaborations with the powers of empire and culture. And we are being called to turn around. This little book, written in the midst of Covid-19 lockdown, invites us to stop and take a good hard look at ourselves and at who Jesus calls us to be as the church.

Jesus is not recorded as saying anything about the church being the purity police or a large company or a social club. Instead, Jesus, the radiant One, talks about followers being little, like salt and branches and infants. The imagery Jesus weaves together is of being pockets of dynamic grace through whom Spirit can breathe, communities in which all (including ourselves) can discover and share the healing and freedom and meaning that emerges as we draw closer to the Source of all. This is the One who dares to pitch tent among us in Jesus, awakening us to the flow of the kingdom and in whom we discover home.

When people assume that the church is dying, they are often comparing reminiscences about the church of the past with what is before their eyes now. While this may appear to be a logical line to draw, in making this comparison, context is often ignored. It is true that in various decades of the 1900s, and particularly in years following the Second World War, congregations and Sunday schools were full to overflowing. Churches had choirs and social dances (at least the Presbyterians did), and church tennis clubs proliferated. For those old enough to remember this period, I can imagine how easy it is to assume that with almost empty Sunday schools, tennis courts sold off and many vacant pews, the conclusion is obvious – the church is dying. However, if we scratch the surface just a little, we discover a far more complex and interesting reality.

At the outset, it is important to note that in any span of history, there will always be people who long for the divine and who seek to engage with questions of meaning and purpose. Yet, the context in which churches and Sunday schools were full and the church had tennis clubs and social dances last century, emerged out of a very particular set of circumstances. Churches were large in this Western cultural context at a time when people sought to recover from not one, but two, World Wars and (some) sought greater meaning in light of this horrendous experience.

However, there was more at play than the search for meaning. In this period, the societal expectation was that you had to go to church to be a respectful citizen. Church attendance was entwined with cultural assumptions about being a good woman, a trusted businessman or worthy politician. Going to church was linked with imagery of being proper: wearing gloves and hats, not swearing and never overindulging. The non-biblical statement 'cleanliness is next to Godliness' became a kind of proof text for the church's authority as the purveyor of decency.[1] The social pressure to conform was significant, particularly when the voice of the church was often aligned with the state, and seen as the ultimate moral authority.

Added to cultural equations of church with respectability, on a practical level, without televisions, with few cars, with no internet access and with less entertainment options, compared with now, there were far fewer opportunities to connect and socialise. There were fewer places to meet a potential partner, to share in affordable recreation and to make business connections. Churches played an important cultural role in society. Churches were often full and, for many, at the centre of social life. While this, in and of itself, is not wrong, I do not recall Jesus saying that the role of followers – the church – was to build tennis courts, create entertainment hubs or improve social etiquette.

---

[1] This phrase is recorded in a sermon by John Wesley *Sermon 88 On Dress*. Within this sermon, Wesley discusses modest clothing at length and emphasises that money spent on extravagant dress could be money given to the poor. Interestingly, within this sermon, Wesley suggests that it is permissible for those of wealthier classes to dress in more elaborate ways.

While assumptions about church attendance and being proper persist for some, as evidenced in stereotypes of church goers in film and tv, the irony is that this is far removed from what we are told about Jesus' own reputation in the Gospels. Jesus – frankly, and unapologetically – states that he has a reputation for being a party goer: a glutton, a drunkard and a friend of all the 'wrong' sorts people (see Matthew 11:19; Luke 7:34). Indeed, because Jesus consistently chooses to spend time feasting with, and befriending, improper people, 'sinners and tax collectors', the respectable religious leaders of Jesus' day are utterly appalled and perplexed (see Matthew 9:11-13; Mark 2:13-17; Luke 5:27-32).

We are living through times of rapid change. In a few short decades, the assumption that being part of the church is an essential ingredient for garnering respectability has flipped. Indeed, in many places, the very opposite is now true. In the Australian context, if someone discovers you are a Christian, you are likely to be viewed with suspicion or derision or both. In part, this is due to the exposure of the hideous behaviour of people with authority in the worldwide church who have perpetrated abuse against children. This is compounded by the persistent and arrogant denial of this abuse, or its seriousness, in some church denominations. The deep, and valid, mistrust of the church – and of Christians – is only reinforced by those people of Christian faith who violently oppose and condemn other people who are simply getting on with their lives. This is reflected in some Christian traditions' condemnation of women who experience God's call to ministry, or in the exclusion of people who love Jesus and are part of the LGBTQI community.

And while many churches – including Uniting Church congregations – are not like this, often it is the most judgmental and negative church voices that attract media attention. To put this bluntly, over the last century, what was a form of cultural 'compulsory voting' church attendance has now become an optional, and, for many a questionable, choice. This is the context in which we find ourselves.

What I find intriguing about this change in society is not that pews are empty, but that people still choose to attend church at all. People are clearly not doing this for kudos or respect in the Australian context anymore. In addition to this, there are plenty of affordable, quality entertainment options available that do not involve giving up Sunday mornings. People now have a plethora of ways to connect with others and to promote their businesses. However, despite the flack and the diverse opportunities on offer, young and old people are still keen to find out about the way of Jesus and to go deeper. My sense is that while numbers may be lower, the actual number of people who are part of church communities because they are seeking to be disciples of Jesus (not join the tennis club, or be seen to be a respectable citizen, or to gain more votes) may be higher.

Without realising it, metaphors shape our lives and create meaning for us. Dominant metaphors for the church, for more than a millennium, have been large. In hymn, art and architecture, the church has been imaged as triumphant, as an army and as the overbearing stronghold in the town square, arbitrating value, belonging and respectability. Instead of assuming that we know what the church is for and what a successful church looks like, in the pages that follow we will return to investigate a metaphor that Jesus uses in the Gospels. In doing so, we will seek to disentangle empire-shaped versions of Christianity that are commonly entwined with notions of respectability and cultural success, from the call of Jesus.

The Beatitudes, recorded in both Matthew and Luke, are well known (Matthew 5:1-12; Luke 6:20-26). In Matthew's Gospel, just after Jesus proclaims these disruptive words in which it is disclosed that the dreamings of God reside with the poor in spirit, the meek, the merciful and the peacemakers – not the rich, the dominating or violent, Jesus goes on to say 'you are the salt of the earth' (Matthew 5:13). The imagery of being salt is curious. While empire-shaped metaphors of the church have dominated imagination, song and art, there are not many hymns, liturgies, art works or buildings that engage with this metaphor of being salty.

What might it mean for the church to be salt? This metaphor has a multiplicity of potential implications. Staying with this imagery, and attending to its various threads, may help us to break free from the lies we have told ourselves about being church. Salt is tiny. Salt is in our tears and wombs, cleansing, healing and growing up life. Salt preserves. Salt seasons, amplifying taste. And, importantly, when we have too much salt, it spoils our food and health. In the pages that follow, we seek to consider the ways in which we may have lost our salty taste (Matthew 5:13) and we will wrestle and play with this metaphor of being salt as we seek to reflect on how Jesus may be calling us to be church today.

To accompany us on this journey of discovery, we will take some time to listen to the biblical text and to walk alongside early church writers. While the circumstances of early church writers are very different from ours, there are some striking similarities that may yet bear fruit in helping us to reflect upon our context. This is particularly the case for those who wrote before the church became entwined with the state. Finally, we will spend time with congregations that are not dying but are growing; and explore what they are doing and why they are doing it.

A word of warning at the outset. This is not a 'how to' manual for church success. This is not a book of stories about how struggling churches made three simple changes and then vast numbers of people flooded into their buildings. Not only would this be reducing the Christian faith to a pyramid selling scheme, equating big numbers with faithfulness or growth, we would be yet again falling for our culture's lies about what success is. Instead, we are going to dive into the hard space of discomfort as we unravel assumptions about church and seek to engage genuinely with the question of what the marks of Christian faithfulness and growth might actually be.

Wondering Questions

What images traditionally come to mind for you when you think about the church?

What strikes you about the metaphor of the church being salt?

What questions and thoughts emerge for you after reading this chapter?

How would you draw or imagine the church as salt?

Reflection and Prayer Resources

Light a candle.

Spend some time reflecting alone, or with your community, on the wondering questions.

Rest in some silence.

Pray the Lord's prayer – remembering that the type of kingdom that Jesus speaks about is like a mustard seed, a feast for the marginalised and like a woman looking for a lost coin – and is thus very different from the kingdoms of this world.

Chapter Two

The littleness of salt

When we assume that a successful church – one that is not dying – is characterised by large numbers of people filling our vast buildings, at least two things are happening. First, we are assuming that the church of the recent past is the norm, without critically engaging with the question of why numbers have been so high. Second, we are accepting the assumptions of empire and consumerist culture that equate size with success, without critical analysis. The assumption that the church must be large in order to be successful or faithful is curious when it is brought before the metaphor of being like salt. Salt is not large or imposing, instead, salt is made up of tiny grains.

Christian writers from a time when the church was not large and not successful, according to this limited criteria, lend us wisdom and perspective in our own context. Or, at the least, they provide us with informed and faithful conversation partners. Justin, who was to become known as Justin Martyr after he was killed for his Christian faith, was born around 100 C.E. At the time of his birth, John's Gospel may not have yet been written and Mark, Matthew and Luke's Gospels were likely only a few decades old. Christian communities were not large. Church buildings did not yet exist and, significantly,

Christians were regarded very suspiciously by both the state and the wider community. Justin's eloquent writing is some of the earliest Christian writing we have outside the Second Testament canon.[2] He was a Gentile and deeply committed to seeking meaning and purpose in life. Before becoming a Christian, Justin explored various philosophical schools and writes about his experiences of these in his *Dialogue with Trypho*.

In Justin's letter entitled the *First Apology*, addressed to the Emperor (*1 Apology* 1), he seeks to defend Christians from unfair treatment by the government and from community disdain. Within this letter, we gain insight not only into Justin's theology, but also into the nature of the widespread view of Christians. As it turns out, one of the central accusations leveled at the very early church is that they are atheists. Justin writes:

> Thus we are even called atheists. We do proclaim ourselves atheists as regards those whom you call gods, but not with respect to the Most True God, who is alien to all evil and is the Father of justice, temperance, and the other virtues. (*1 Apology* 6)

In Justin's context, Christians are being accused of being atheists because they refuse to go along with predominant

---

[2] The term 'Second' Testament is preferred to 'New' Testament. This is because the language of 'New' Testament can imply that the Christian canon replaces the older, Jewish canon. This is not the case. For Christians, our faith is grounded upon, and indebted to, Jewish texts and traditions. While not without issues, the language of First Testament and Second Testament is utilised in this work.

cultural and religious practices. In particular, they are not making offerings to the plethora of local gods. This was a serious issue at the time because people held (and, perhaps, leaders stoked) deep concerns about the ramifications of these Christians' anti-civic behaviour in refusing to make sacrifices.

It is difficult for us to fathom the level of hatred and fear such refusal brought within the wider community. But at the time, wildly unpredictable Graeco-Roman gods were seen as a very real threat. These gods could punish whole communities at will, through any number of natural disasters. Christians refusing to make offerings to these gods was tantamount to inviting catastrophe. Despite this, Justin is unrepentant about the refusal of Christians to go along with cultural and religious expectations:

> We do not worship with many sacrifices and floral offerings the things humans have made, set in temples, and called gods... This we think is not only stupid but also disrespectful to God, who is of ineffable glory and form. (*1 Apology* 9)

The consequences for Christians were significant. Rather than garnering respect for their beliefs, in this context, Christians invited mistrust and hatred. We get a sense of the level of animosity directed at Christians in one of Justin's asides in the Second Apology:

> Lest anyone should say to us, 'All of you, go, kill yourselves and thus go immediately to God, and save us the trouble', I will explain why we do not do that, and why, when interrogated, we boldly acknowledge our faith. (*2 Apology* 4)

While in the Australian context, being a Christian no longer invites respect or trust, we are not usually at risk of people wishing us all dead. This is an important point to underscore. In Australia (and the West more generally), while Christianity is no longer located at the centre of society, and the church is no longer a symbol of respectability or authority, it would be a lie to suggest that we are persecuted. This is not the case everywhere around the world, of course. In some places, being a Christian does mean risking one's life, as reflected, for example, in attacks in recent years upon churches in Indonesia and Egypt and in the persecution of Christians in Iran. In drawing attention to Justin's statements, it is not being suggested that Christians in Australia are under attack. Instead, it is being underscored that the church has not always been large or respected by society or the state and, importantly, these are not the marks of Christian success or faithfulness.

Within Justin's context of being part of a small and maligned faith community, we gain important insight into what he understands to be core to Christian faith. For Justin, large numbers are not a marker of success. Church buildings are entirely irrelevant. Community respect is not expected, and government support or protection is a very distant hope. According to Justin, in this context of being small and maligned, what is core to being a successful and faithful church is how Christians live. Drawing deeply from the Sermon on the Mount, Justin explains:

> The heavenly Father wishes the repentance of a sinner, rather than their punishment. Concerning the love we should have for all, Christ thus taught: 'If you love those

who love you, what new thing do you do? For even the fornicators do this. But I say unto you, pray for your enemies, love them that hate you, bless them that curse you, and pray for them who insult you'. He taught us to share our goods with the needy and to do nothing for our own personal glory, when he said, 'Give to everyone who asks of you, and do no turn your back on anyone who would borrow; for if you lend to them who you hope will repay you, what new things do you do?' And 'Be kind and merciful as your heavenly Father also is kind and merciful, who makes his sun to rise on sinners, and on the just and the wicked'. (*1 Apology* 15)

For Justin, living in radical generosity is core to the successful practice of Christian faith. This is not simply because Christians values are a nice idea but, informed by Jesus' words in the Sermon on the Mount, because this reflects who and how God is.

Justin goes on to talk about the impacts of Christians living out their faith in this way upon their neighbours. After talking about living in non-retaliation, and again quoting the Sermon on the Mount, Justin points out that:

We can show that this happened in the case of many of those who were of your side and turned from a life of violence and tyranny, because they were conquered either by the constancy of their neighbours' lives, or by the strange patience they noticed in their injured associates or by experiencing their honesty in business matters. (*1 Apology* 16)

For Justin, seeking to live into Jesus' disclosure and embodiment of who and how God is – merciful, non-violent and compassionate – and thus seeking to be likewise generous, loving and non-retaliatory towards all, is integral to Christian faith. Numbers, buildings, worship-as-entertainment, being relevant, gaining community admiration or government respect, or meeting an abstract growth criteria are not core to being a faithful church. Interestingly, Justin points out that the accumulative impact of Christians embodying the compassion of Christ in their everyday lives, sprinkled across the community, is that people are encountering the good news and their lives are being transformed.

For Justin, embodying the love of Christ is not the only aspect of the church being successful or faithful. Worship is also integral. Justin gives us rare insight into very early Christian worship. He is writing at a time before hierarchies have been solidified, liturgies fixed, and massive buildings erected. At the time, wild rumours were beginning to spread about what Christians did in worship. Far removed from more recent notions of the church being the signifier of all things respectable, in the second century not only were Christians accused of being atheists, stories also abounded that Christians shared in cannibalistic feasts in their worship.[3] In the face of such misrepresentation, Justin spells out what Christian worship is about:

---

[3] Both Justin Martyr (*Dialogue* 10) and Tertullian (*Ad Nationes* 1.7; cf. *Apology* 7 and 8) speak of the accusation that Christians are cannibals.

On the day that is called Sunday, we have a common assembly of all who live in the cities or in the outlying districts, and the memoirs of the Apostles or the writings of the prophets are read, as long as there is time. Then when the reader has finished, the president of the assembly verbally admonishes and invites all to imitate such examples of virtue. Then we all stand up together and offer up our prayers, and, as we said before, after we finish our prayers, bread and wine and water are presented. The one who presides likewise offers up prayers and thanksgivings, to the best of their ability, and the people express their approval by saying 'Amen'. (1 Apology 67)

Justin goes on to explain that for those who cannot make it to worship, deacons distribute the bread and wine after the service. Justin also underscores the importance of generosity not only within daily life, but also within the context of Christian worship:

The wealthy, if they wish, contribute whatever they desire, and the collection is placed in the custody of the president and this is used to help the orphans and widows and those who are needy because of sickness or any other reason, and the captives and strangers in our midst. (1 Apology 67)

Justin shows no interest in the impressiveness of worship. His aside that the presiders pray 'to the best of their ability' seems to imply that these prayers are not always polished or perfect. Worship is simple and seeks to be authentic and generous. The core elements of worship, according to Justin, are attending to, and engaging with, writings that would become part of Christian sacred scripture, praying together and being nourished by Christ Jesus, the compassionate, crucified, risen and present One in bread, wine and water. Nurtured by this gathering in worship, these maligned people of the Way, Christ-Ones, were emboldened to disperse across the city and region back to their homes, embodying the divine's generosity with their neighbours, enemies and strangers during the week.

The vital connection between experiencing Christ's love and sharing this love with others is important to underscore. Worship is not a duty, performance, or forum for a social club. Instead, worship is primarily the place of, together, communing with and being fed by Christ, the face of God. In a text written in the first century by the church in Rome to the church in Corinth, likely before Justin was even born, the connection between experiencing Christ's love and the practice of generosity is made plain. The authors state:

> The one who experiences love in Christ should do what Christ commanded. Who can explain the bond of God's love? Who is able to recount the greatness of its beauty? The height to which love leads is beyond description... Everyone chosen by God has been perfected in love; apart from love nothing is pleasing to God. (*1 Clement* 49:1-5)

Experience the love of Christ and share this love. This is the call for Christians in this first century text. This is also the pattern of Christian life for Justin.

It is no accident that these same marks of the church are central attributes in the Uniting Church's description of the purpose of the congregation as described within The

Basis of Union. In the *Basis*, it is stated that core to being a congregation is gathering in worship to be nourished by sacred text and sacraments, building one another up in this love and then going out to share this divine love in the world:

> The Congregation is the embodiment in one place of the One Holy Catholic and Apostolic Church, worshipping, witnessing and serving as a fellowship of the Spirit in Christ. Its members meet regularly to hear God's Word, to celebrate the sacraments, to build one another up in love, to share in the wider responsibilities of the Church, and to serve the world. (*Basis of Union*, para 15)

I wonder how different our churches might be if we saw this as the core work of being the church? If our energy was not spent on striving for large numbers, shiny worship, popular programs, being relevant, or cultivating on-trend mission statements, who might we be then? Without the pressure of keeping up appearances, I wonder if, perhaps, nourishment and joy might flow more freely, both into our lives together as a church and through us out to others.

In our current context of the COVID-19 pandemic, many of the 'normal' things that define church practice are no longer able to happen. We cannot gather together in buildings, we cannot sing together, we cannot have social clubs in person or run outreach programs face to face. We cannot share together in Eucharist, or Holy Communion, in person. We cannot even share a cup of tea together. What does the very early church have to teach us about being the church right now? This is the thing. The call to live in generosity, to care for our neighbours and for strangers, to give to those in need and to pray for those opposed to us, all of this is still possible. Likewise, the call to worship together as we wrestle with sacred text and pray together – as we are nourished by Christ Jesus – all of these things are also possible within lockdown and beyond.[4]

For Justin, and the members of churches in Rome and Corinth in the first century, being a Christian is about being part of little Jesus communities dotted around a hostile empire, living within a wider community that is often suspicious and antagonistic. These realities are not a mark of church decline. They are a given. The priority of these early church communities is not to improve their social standing or increase their brand recognition. Instead, they focus on what is core – experiencing and sharing the love of Christ Jesus, Emmanuel, God-with-us, the Holy One who is kind.

In contemporary context, if we too chose to put down the idols that church success and faithfulness are equated with cultural respect and size, and, instead, focus our energy on experiencing and embodying Christ's love, this may free us and energise us. Ironically, this may also let neighbours, strangers and enemies with whom our lives our enmeshed, taste a little of the healing, spiciness of the divine who comes to us in Christ.

A little congregation

I could paint a picture of the congregation I currently serve according to the success criteria of our culture. I could tell

---

[4] The *Basis of Union* rightly emphasises that we are nourished by Christ Jesus not only in Holy Communion: 'On the way Christ feeds the Church with Word and Sacraments, and it has the gift of the Spirit in order that it may not lose the way' (*Basis of Union*, para 3).

you, with great flourish, that since I arrived, the church has more than tripled in size and the predominant age group of new comers is those in their twenties and thirties. While this is true, this is not the whole story. When I arrived at Richmond Uniting, there were around twelve people attending. More than tripling these numbers does not make for a large congregation. Furthermore, many of the people who connect with Richmond Uniting find it difficult to attend worship, or other church gatherings, regularly. Some cannot commit to leadership roles. Though, given space and time, it is moving to see younger and 'newer' people choosing to take up leadership positions and share their expertise.

While there is much vitality at Richmond Uniting, in many ways we continue to travel through unpredictable valleys. There are multiple reasons for this. A significant factor is that many people who attend this congregation have been through church trauma in other traditions. Others are exploring Christian faith for the very first time. Some have been told by parents, or church leaders, that they are bound for hell because they are gay. Others are trying to make sense of what faith might look like, and how they might approach the Bible, if it is not the literal 'word of God'. Others are dealing with mental health issues, highly demanding jobs or full-time study, and some are living through the heartbreaking reality of being on temporary visas, never knowing when they, or loved ones, might be sent back to unsafe countries that they have fled. Some people have been serving the church faithfully for six decades, or longer, and are getting tired.

People who are part of Richmond Uniting have a lot going on in their lives. Simply making it to worship amidst life's challenges, let alone attending to the 'regular' demands of life and study and work and unemployment, is rather impressive. I suspect many people across diverse congregations and denominations are living through the same kind of realities.

If we were to look at Richmond, and congregations like Richmond, according to the criteria of the church of the last century, with success predicated on large numbers, choirs and various social groups, it would be deemed a failure. However, if success is based on what Justin thinks is core to Christian faithfulness and success – sharing God's kindness and generosity with neighbour and enemy; and worshipping, praying and engaging with Christian sacred texts to be nourished by Christ – we might see things a little differently.

Each year at Richmond Uniting (before COVID-19), we gather for an evening called Pizza Dreaming. We reflect on the previous year and lean in to listen to one another's dreamings about the following year and eat pizza together. We also hope to listen for God's dreamings for the congregation. The questions we ask of ourselves are not 'did we like worship?' or 'what would make us more trendy?' Instead, we reflect on what has helped worship to be a space for authentic transformative encounter with God and what hindered this; what has helped to create space to engage with and go more deeply into the way of Jesus and what has hindered this, and how have we lived simply, generously and creatively, serving in our local and global village and what has hindered this. We also spend time reflecting together on what new ways we might live into these core goals.

Worship as transformative encounter with God

In worship at Richmond Uniting, we don't have a band, or Power Point slides. We don't seek to be 'on trend', but we do seek to shut up and listen for God, giving space for Spirit to move and speak, within and among us. We don't dumb down the Bible. We do, however, seek to wrestle with the complexity and beauty of the Bible and theology in the midst of real life. At our most recent Pizza Dreaming event, people underscored what made worship both authentic and transformative for them. Elements people highlighted included:

> ... silence, space to reflect, stopping and slowing down, reflections (sermons) that spoke about the Bible, culture and context, not shying away from difficult topics, giving cues/rubrics about the flow of worship and learning from one another within worship.

A few years ago, the congregation read the book *Take This Bread* by Sarah Miles. Flowing from discussions afterwards, the congregation decided to begin worshipping over a meal once a month. In this worship, we gather in the early evening instead of the morning. We push all the pews back, worshipping around one long communal table in the middle of the church. Sometimes this worship is amazing. Sometimes the conversation is stilted. People who would never normally spend time together, the tattooed Goth and the retired principal, the refugee, the uni student and the young children sit side by side, sharing Jesus' bread and wine and simple vegetarian soup. We share in conversation about Jesus and the Bible readings, we wrestle with the implications of the text, we sing unaccompanied, we light candles and pray together.

When we gather for worship, whether it be in this evening worship over a meal or in 'normal' Sunday morning worship, we seek to authentically welcome everyone who walks through the door – regardless of their lifestyle, age, cultural background, poverty or wealth, their hair colour or the number of piercings they have.

Leaning into the way of Jesus (or, can I get a witness?)

At Richmond Uniting, we also seek to deeply explore Christian faith in an ongoing way. This exploration occurs during worship in teaching and discussion, in book groups, in Creed Conversations for those preparing for baptism or confirmation and in our monthly 'Lingering Lunch' conversations after church. We also share links to podcasts, articles and films that explore theology, spirituality or the Bible.

In addition to this, we occasionally host one-off seminars both for those within and beyond the church community. These seminars intentionally create opportunities for people to 'dip in' to questions of Christian faith and spirituality, but with no strings attached. Topics have included 'children and spirituality' and 'why creationism isn't biblical'. These stand-alone seminars are a form of 'witness' that provide authentic points of engagement with the wider community, while at the same time respecting that people are on their own journey. People may choose to explore Christian faith further with us or we may never see them again. We offer these events as a gift, without seeking to control the outcomes.

However, there is an ongoing tension in offering these opportunities within and beyond the congregation. Many people are keen to attend but are time poor. On top of this, many people live far from the congregation, and for those who do live closer finding parking is difficult and travelling alone at night in Richmond can be an issue of safety. Others are hindered from participating due to all kinds of challenges that they are facing. Face to face weekly Bible study groups, or 'cell' groups, that may have thrived a few decades ago, have not worked in this inner city community.

That said, one of the strange gifts of COVID-19 lockdown is that it has brought new ways of doing things. Quite unexpectedly, a new Theology Thursday group has emerged with a small group of people meeting weekly online to discuss theology and the themes that have emerged in worship on the previous Sunday. As well as this, a new Midday Prayer service has been able to begin online, with people joining in from home or work to pray together. The irony is that with the physical doors of the church being closed, more inclusive ways of being church have emerged. These new patterns have enabled people currently living interstate, and older people for whom night travel can be difficult, to participate meaningfully.

While new technologies are emerging as important gifts for the whole church, the issue of people being time poor is still a dominant reality for many. This is an issue that is not unique to Richmond Uniting. This kind of scenario is increasingly common across congregations and denominations. When people lament the fact that the church used to thrive on small groups, Bible study groups and community groups, and when it is suggested that people lack commitment these days, crucial context is forgotten. Decades ago, when such groups thrived, most households had one full time person at home, usually a woman, caring for children, managing bills and carrying the 'mental load' of maintaining a household. Both women and men, one confined to unpaid work in the home, one confined to paid work out of the home, had the time and, I suspect, relished the space, to be out and part of such groups.

This context is very far removed from reality now. If people are partnered and have children, most commonly both parents work and so the stresses of managing a household and caring for children are juggled within the ongoing demands of employment. It is not the case that people now lack commitment. Instead, the reality is that people have far less of one of the most precious commodities there is in life – time.

At Richmond Uniting, we seek to honour our littleness and peoples' busyness and adapt to do what we can do, without resorting to shaming people. Rather than the dissipation of face to face small groups or church run community groups being understood as a failing, perhaps this is a further point of contact with the very early church and a hint about the way forward for an increasing number of congregations whose issues reflect those at Richmond. In the church community Justin is part of, people paused to meet together on Sundays amidst the struggles and precariousness of living in the Roman empire. According to Justin, this Sunday gathering is *the* essential point of contact for these early Christians and the context in which Christ nourished them to go out, week by week, to live out the love of Christ for all.

The slur 'Sunday Christians' used by some, implies that people are not living out their faith – and thus not at mission – during the week in the rest of their lives. To fall for this kind of thinking is to assume that the 'mission of the church' can only happen through official church programs. This denies both the gifts and faithfulness of Christians being at mission in the whole of their lives, as Justin points to. This also seeks to contain the work of Spirit who, Jesus makes plain, moves where she will (John 3:5-8).

Living simply, generously and creatively, serving in our local and global village

At Richmond Uniting, alongside worshipping and witnessing, we seek to live simply and generously, serving locally, nationally and internationally in a variety of ways. We seek to do this in our own lives, as well as a congregation. We also seek to create space to continue to discuss how we might live in this way and what blocks compassion in our lives, day to day.

As a congregation in the inner city, where many people face drug and alcohol addiction issues, we have been local advocates for the trialing of a Medically Supervised Injecting Centre. The congregation also runs an ecumenical Food Centre together with our Anglican and Roman Catholic brothers and sisters. Many congregational members volunteer at this Food Centre, others donate food, and as a congregation we help to finance this project.

We provide low-cost housing to a refugee family. We also support the work of Boroondara Community Outreach, a Uniting Church mental health program in Melbourne and a *UnitingWorld* water sanitation project in Papua New Guinea. We have recently begun supporting a theological scholarship program in the Pacific, a program initiated through *UnitingWorld*, through a bequest that we are responsible for stewarding.

We don't have an op shop or run a soup kitchen. We don't run a drop-in centre during the week. We haven't worked out how to most effectively advocate to government for better housing for people experiencing homelessness. I share these examples of how we serve, not in the effort to prove our worth, or impress with our efforts. Caring is not a competition. When we slip in to competing, this is a sure sign that we are not anchored in Christ. Other congregations will be doing more. We are little, and to some extent fragile, but we are seeking to be faithful to the core issues of being church, as we seek to worship the Holy One-Sacred Three authentically and journey more deeply with Christ and to love our neighbours and enemies (I often remind the congregation of the need to pray for all politicians, not just those we agree with). We also continue to prayerfully discern how best to do all of this.

One of the challenging things about being a church that is trying to live into this early church success criteria that Jesus proclaims in the Sermon on the Mount, and that Justin underscores, is that it is not shiny or easily boasted about. In our culture that thrives on big numbers and virtue signaling, success based on seeking to faithfully gather for worship, being kind and generous to all and praying for those who we disagree with, or who hate us, doesn't translate easily into a popular tweet or into cultural or collegial kudos. Furthermore, this work is never complete. If we approach worship, or loving neighbour and enemy like a 'to do' list that leads to some ultimately successful outcome, we are likely to burn out or become bitter.

In the Sermon on the Mount, Jesus proclaims that being merciful and kind and loving are core, not because we will be successful, or the world will value these things (indeed, Jesus is clear that the world will likely hate us – Matthew 5:11-12). Jesus doesn't even promise that this will finally fix the state of the world. Instead, we are called into this merciful kindness, because this reflects divine reality (Matthew 5:43-48). When we live focused on the God who comes to us in Christ, experiencing and sharing love, hopefully we will begin to realise that we will never get the 'job done' and that this is not the goal. Instead, as Christians we are called into a far more vulnerable way of being – tasting and sharing the good reality at the heart of the universe that is poured out for all things.

In order to enter and sustain this pattern of life that is shaped by open generosity and prayer and leaning into Jesus' teaching and nourishment, we need to put down the assumption that there is some ultimate outcome that we will eventually achieve. We also need to rely a little more heavily on God's energy and learn to rest. This is far more likely, I suspect, when we reclaim the reality that core to being the church is being little pockets of compassion who are reliant upon nourishment from the Source of all.

Worship and service go together for us Christians. In allowing ourselves to repeatedly, week by week, come back to the mat, to the feet of Christ Jesus and to let ourselves be washed and fed, we are emboldened for grace. In this practice, we are invited, again and again, to step off the treadmill of the lies of our culture: self-reliance, accomplishment and proving our worth via our achievements, and into a whole new way of being grounded in divine homecoming. In order to enter this, we need to relinquish our desire to be successful, big or impactful and instead engage with the sacred ordinary work of being saturated in divine grace in the middle of our messy lives and sharing this without keeping score.

Demons

Before we turn to reflect on a different dimension of Jesus' metaphor of salt, it is important to highlight another aspect of Justin's theology. Throughout Justin's writing, he is clear that he expects that there will be hostility. Like so many others in the Common Era, Justin's cosmic world view is that that there are demons who are actively thwarting the dreamings of God (see, for example, *First Apology* 26; 56; 57; 58; *Dialogue with Trypho* 82). While we may no longer share this kind of cosmology, Justin's worldview is a useful challenge to our naiveté. There continue to be many powers and forces that push against the way of Christ. These include racism, individualism, consumerism, class-based prejudice, the seductiveness of 'cancel culture' that dominates the social media landscape right now, as well as mob mentality fear.

If we take seriously that the call of Christ to love neighbour and enemy is integral, racism has no place. We cannot exclude or devalue people because of their cultural background, because all people are children of God. If we take seriously Jesus' words that God loves with indiscriminate abandon, bringing rain on the just and the unjust (Matthew 5:43-48), we can no longer fall for the constant pressure of endless competing in order to prove our worth.

If we take Jesus seriously about living in radical generosity (see Matthew 25:31-46), we can no longer fall for the lies of endless consumption because we are called to share our resources, giving away as much as we can to those in need. We cannot deride or dismiss those who have a different opinions to us, including politicians, because we are called to love them and pray for them. Endlessly, we Christians are called out of fear into the freedom of love by Spirit (see Romans 8:14-17).

To live as Christians is to attract the wrath and disdain of all these forces in our society. As it turns out, when churches are faithful to the call of Christ they will often find themselves not at the centre of society, but on the edges – feasting and loving alongside Jesus with all kinds of people we might not normally spend time with, and, like Jesus, copping derision for being there and living like this. We just need to remember that, despite the various toxic forces at work, this is not a sign of our failure, but of following Christ.

Wondering Questions

What strikes you most as you read this chapter?

How do you react to what Justin thinks is core to being church?

How do you respond to the idea of the faithful church being little and focused on the work of experiencing the love of Christ and sharing this love with neighbour, stranger and enemy?

Reflection and Prayer Resources

It will take hard work – and I suspect – deep spiritual work to break free from the dominant assumptions that church success equates with big numbers, large buildings and shiny worship-as-entertainment.

Light a candle.

Spend some time reflecting alone, or with your community, on the wondering questions.

Hold some grains of salt in your hand.

Rest in some silence.

Close with the following prayer:

Jesus, bright morning star,
You say we are salt –
the salt of the earth.
Forgive us when we would rather be an army.
Set us free from our longings for crowds and castles.
Tear down our walls and tear up our to-do lists.
Help us to rest in the palm of your hand
as we are
little grains of salt – each one of us – beloved.
Help us to let you hold us
so that we can uncoil.
Help us to relax into our smallness and trust in your vastness
so that together we may become pockets of compassion – as
you call us to be.
Amen.

Chapter Three

Salty tears

When we cry, we taste our inherent saltiness. What might the metaphor of being salt, like tears, mean for the church? In earliest Christian traditions tears have an important place. Jesus wept. This is the shortest verse in the Bible (John 11:35). While punctuation was added later to Greek manuscripts and we cannot know with certitude why editors chose to isolate these particular words to form their own brief sentence, I am glad that these editors did. In this short statement, a world of theology resides. Christians share the conviction that, somehow, God comes to us in Jesus. Here, disrupting all kinds of superman images of God, we encounter the God One who is vulnerable. This is the Holy One who does not stand aloof from our pain but who enters into our suffering. More than even that, this Holy One is not simply a bystander witnessing our grief, instead this One enters into our tears with us, as so tenderly described in John's Gospel when Lazarus lies in the grave and Jesus weeps with Martha and Mary (John 11). Ours is the God who weeps with us as we weep. In reclaiming the place of tears in church, we may discover healing life.

Unlike our culture that doggedly tells us to 'be positive', in the early church tears are assumed to have a place. Not only do tears have a place, tears and grief are honoured as an expression of faithfulness and a part of the journey of faith. In reading the Gospels as a whole we are left in no doubt of the integral place of tears for Jesus. In the garden, on the night of Jesus' betrayal, Jesus' deep grief and suffering are given vivid expression (see Matthew 26:36-46; Mark 14:32-42; Luke 22:39-46). As graphically described in Matthew and Mark, on the cross not only does Jesus experience the betrayal of friends, the brutality of an unjust legal system and agonising physical violence, Jesus also experiences the absence of divine presence. Drawing from Psalm 22, Jesus cries from the depths his experience of abandonment – 'My God, my God why have you forsaken me?' (Matthew 27:46; Mark 15:34).

Tears are not simply assumed to be acceptable for Jesus. Tears are understood to be part of the ongoing journey of Christian discipleship. Illustrating this, rather than encouraging people to 'be positive' or 'get over it', Paul has this simple and profound advice for the Jesus community in Rome:

> Rejoice with those who rejoice, weep with those who weep (Romans 12:15).

Here, Paul encourages this embryotic Jesus community to be like Jesus, who weeps with us. Indeed, throughout this portion of Paul's letter, the community is invited to mirror Jesus' non-violent love, compassion and *bearing with* generosity (Romans 12:9-21).

The valid and valued place of tears is also underscored in a different portion of Second Testament text. Within Revelation, the dreamscape writings of John the Revelator, a vision is cast in which God bears witness to peoples' tears and tends to them:

> For the Lamb at the centre of the throne will be their shepherd,
> and he will guide them to springs of the water of life,
> and God will wipe away every tear from their eyes.
> (Revelation 7:17)

The evocative imagery of God tending peoples' tears is returned to in the penultimate chapter of this text (Revelation 21:4).

As well as calling people in the church in Rome to weep – like Jesus – with those who weep, in this letter Paul is also honest about how difficult life can be. Instead of pretending that everything is perfect because they are all now Christians, Paul names the kinds of suffering that people are enduring as they follow Christ. According to Paul, this includes hardship, distress, persecution, famine, nakedness, peril and the sword (Romans 8:35). Within such contexts of suffering, tears are surely inevitable.

As Paul spells out so clearly, robust Christian faith is not an exercise in pretending that 'everything is awesome'. Entering into relationship with Christ Jesus, the God of the tears, and allowing our lives to become interwoven with this life of the divine is a costly invitation into facing and naming reality, including our sorrow, and letting the tears, the grief and the questions flow. Despite the positive thinking mantras of our culture, and some churches, we are not failing at faith and life when sorrow weighs us down. In contrast, these tears can be the gift that paradoxically births space for authentic joy and healing to emerge.

The profound place of tears is not only named in Second Testament texts, but also affirmed within the First Testament. In many sacred stories tears are integral. Joseph weeps so loudly when he is reunited with his brothers, who had sold him into slavery, that Pharaoh's whole household hears (Genesis 45:1-2). Rachel weeps bitterly over the loss of her children. Readers are told that this grief is so immense that she refuses to be comforted (Jeremiah 31:15). The author of Matthew returns to Rachel and her grief when precious babies and infants are mercilessly killed by the state (Matthew 2:16-18). For those who have experienced the agony of losing a baby or child, Rachel's refusal to be comforted rings with a righteous truth. Put away the platitudes. This is a place for tears.

In the Psalms, the importance of tears is also made plain. Alongside beautiful songs and prayers of joy and disturbing tirades of rage, the Psalms give language to lament and grief. Here we discover tears shed within the context of – not separate from – prayer. These ancient liturgical sources have been used for individual and corporate worship for thousands of years by people of both Jewish and Christian faith. However, often in contemporary Christian churches, we do not read, pray or sing the Psalms of sadness. For example, while people may be familiar with the vivid imagery at the beginning of Psalm 42 in which the speaker longs for God like a deer who longs for water, it may be less familiar that this writer goes on to describe being in a state of endless tears:

> As a deer longs for flowing streams,
>   so my soul longs for you, O God.
> My soul thirsts for God,
>   for the living God.
> When shall I come and behold
>   the face of God?
> My tears have been my food
>   day and night,
> while people say to me continually,
>   'Where is your God?' (Psalm 42:1-3)

Without apology or shame, this writer's prayer simply states the truth of his (or her) experience 'my tears have been my food day and night'.

In another Psalm, the constancy of tears is also given vivid expression. In Psalm 6, the author writes:

> I am weary with my moaning;
>   every night I flood my bed with tears;
>   I drench my couch with my weeping.
> My eyes waste away because of my grief;
>   they grow weak because of all my foes. (Psalm 6: 6-7)

In both these Psalms, which are ardent prayers to God, the experience of being bathed in tears is not understood as a sign of a lack of faith or a failing of strength. Instead, the reality of grief and of tears is honestly named and included within the very fabric of prayer.

Psalms 77 and Psalm 88 also speak at length about the experience of the presence of the absence of God as part of – not separate from – being a person of faith. Likewise, Psalm 22 – that Jesus draws from on the cross – speaks agonisingly about the experience of the absence of God. When Paul calls the community in Rome to weep with those who weep, he is drawing not only from testimony about who and how God is revealed to be in Jesus. Paul, who is utterly grounded in Jewish faith and practice, is also drawing from sacred weeping traditions encoded within the Psalms. Indeed, it is these worship resources, the Psalms, that constituted some of the first spiritual songbooks of earliest Jesus communities (see Colossians 3:16).

I'm (not) crying - you're crying

What might it be like for contemporary Jesus communities if church leaders were honest about the kinds of suffering that they, and other people, endure? Imagine if, instead of encouraging one another to always 'be positive', we were safe enough communities for people to talk about the difficulty of losing loved ones, job insecurity, struggles with mental health, being stuck on the destructive treadmill of productivity, or of feeling the absence of God. Imagine if – in church – we were able to weep with one another and pray prayers of lament together without rushing for the tissues or trying to cheer one another up. Imagine if we were able to cultivate courageous friendships in which we did not try and solve each other's 'problems', but instead knew both the power and faithfulness of simply bearing witness to one another's sorrow and the sacred solidarity of sharing in one another's tears. Within this keening space, imagine if we knew in our deep-down beings, that God was weeping with us as we journeyed through shadowy valleys.

In order to engage with such possibilities, Christians and Christian leaders need to do at least three things. One, they need to do the hard work of allowing their own sorrow to surface and their own tears to be wept with God and with the support of others, including professional supports when needed. The importance of this latter point must be underscored. When ministers or church leaders don't do the work of attending to their wounds, but instead dump their wounds on the people they are called to serve, the damage can be irrevocable. In speaking of the important place of tears, I am not speaking of manipulative vulnerability or constructing identities out of victimhood. Nor am I speaking of church communities in which emotions are hyped up or exploited, or in which voyeurism is modelled by leaders and cultivated in congregations. In contrast, I am talking about creating safe spaces in which sorrow can be named and the tears can fall.

Two, in order to be salty communities in which we are able to authentically weep with those who weep, we also need to break free from the absurd lie of our culture that insists that life – and we – should always be positive. There has been a temptation in recent decades, across denominations, for churches to take on our culture's obsession with being positive. To fall in line with this expectation, some churches promise happiness and cultivate beaming smiles and a steady flow of upbeat 'feel good' music. Accompanying this persona, in spoken and unspoken ways, the expectation is made clear that Christians should always be happy. In many places, this trajectory is fuelled by the intertwining of popular 'self-help' positive thinking strategies with Christianity.

There are dangerous byproducts that fall out of this relentless pursuit of happiness. Not only is it inauthentic to pretend to be always happy, this kind of 'pop theology' can very easily lead to devastating consequences for people who dare to be honest about their lives. People who are grieving and people who are journeying with depression or with other mental health issues can end up being blamed for their lack of happiness. In this paradigm, sorrow is equated with faithlessness. The impacts are sometimes life threatening. In order to engage seriously with the call to be a salty church, that is able to weep with those who weep, we need to put down the seductive idol of positivity.

Three, and perhaps this is ironically the most difficult, we need to stop pretending to be messiahs for one another. We are not called to solve one another's lives. We are not God, thankfully. It is church leaders who, perhaps, needs to hear this most of all and most often. By recognising that we are not the messiah, we are more able to do what we are called to do – weep with those who weep. In doing so, we dare to name the truth that life that can be brutal and we dare to embody the reality that we are not saviours, but co-journeyers, with one another as we lean into the transformative energy of God. In doing this, people may yet taste hope. Because when we get out of the way, the God of the tears and the cross, who is also the God of the empty tomb and risen life can move with fresh and surprising healing in her wings.

One of the strange gifts of living in extended lockdown in our worshipping community has been the depth of connection that has been cultivated. Most often, our worship has been in an audio format so that people can dive deeply with God in prayer and sacred text without being fixed to screens. Accompanying this, however, each week we also gather for live 'morning tea' after worship, connecting via our computer screens, phones and tablets. This space, shared gently and with all the technological glitches that weave through this space, including the obligatory call and response: 'you are on mute', 'put your speaker on', has unexpectantly created space for profound solidarity and shared tears. This diverse group of people, whose lives span vastly different lifestyles, cultures and decades, has journeyed with one another in tenderness.

We have literally, some weeks, wept with one another across our loungerooms, as someone has shared the news of an ill loved one, or a life lost, or an awakening to trauma. We have also shared delight in one another's good news and laughed and rejoiced together. On the occasions when there have been tears, it has been humbling, and slightly breathtaking, to witness people not jumping to solve one another's sorrow or push in with inappropriate questions. Instead, people have made space for one another, honouring the tears and simply weeping together. Importantly, amidst the tears, we have also prayed for one another. This has not just been with me, the minister, praying, but across our community and wi-fi connections and living rooms we have all prayed for one another. And I know this prayer has continued to pour out throughout the week across the congregation. In entirely unexpected ways, lockdown has created space for profound connection for our Jesus Community to weep with those who weep and rejoice with those who rejoice.

Rev. Ian David Turnnidge is the Uniting Church minister at the church of St John's on Phillip Island, a rural community south of Melbourne. He can see the sea from his island home, the church manse. Glancing at this congregation's website, it is hard to tell that Ian is their minister. Provocatively, and rather perfectly, on their church website in the space where it states: Minister, instead of Ian's name being written it says this:

Minister: The Members of the Congregation

Ian is not afraid of tears. Some years ago, I remember being struck by his vulnerable words as he presented at a Presbytery meeting, with some eighty people present, to discern whether he was being called to move towards ordination. Instead of sharing a boastful success story, Ian spoke tenderly of recently experiencing the presence of Christ weeping with him, as he journeyed through a season of tears with dear friends who were going through deep loss and who were feeling the presence of the absence of God.

St John's is a growing congregation. Not only are new people joining this church, crucially, people in this community are diving more deeply in their spiritual life and journeying more closely with Christ. Ian is well aware of the societal pressure to be happy, stating 'we live in a culture that just wants to celebrate life and we are not allowed to grieve'. Reflecting on his journey as a minister, and the place of tears in church community, Ian says:

Well, I mean it is what the church does, isn't it? We hold the stories of grief and we allow those stories to have air, and so therefore the grief becomes creative and the grief has a life to it rather than a deadening. So that every, every moment when we offer a prayer or a spaciousness to think of the losses, those we miss and lose, but those who are never really lost to us, they have an opportunity to continue to inform us again, or to allow our faith to reawaken the meanings of those relationships or conversations.

But there is more than this. Beyond the making of meaning in the midst of grief, Ian underscores the call of the church to create space for the truth, even when there is no meaning:

Even in the spaces where... nothing good... can come out of that place, but not even pretending that anything good can come out of it either, but it happened and it's real and it still lives, and it has a place where it can be held and honoured and cherished and nurtured as opposed to being put away or not held.

This is it. Ian is describing a salty church, the Christian faith community as a holding space for tears to flow and for grief to be named and aired, and for truth to be told. At St John's, people in community are doing this in worship, in theology discussion groups and in the wider community, including creating such spaces for truth telling in the local school.

Ian speaks of a recent theological gathering at church in which someone shared that, after a great, gaping loss, for several years this person could not talk to God. This truth was held by those gathered. They knew this was not a problem to solve or a sign of this person's lack of faith. It was the truth that was part of this person's journey of faith. For Ian, it so happened that this courageous sharing in the St John's community hummed with symmetry. That week, Ian had been reflecting on the Gospel reading of Jesus finally getting time to himself after his cousin, John the baptiser, is murdered by the state. When he is able to, Jesus goes up country by himself (see Matthew 14:1-23) and Ian had been pondering that Jesus likely had no words in this prayer space. Sometimes, prayer is wordless, resting on land, walking by the creek, or sitting on the mountain with the sorrow and with God.

Ian and this congregation are being courageous enough to weep together and to wonder together as they cultivate openness to what Spirit is already doing among and within them. They have, thankfully, forsaken the need to be 'positive' or to be the experts. Ian reflects that this way of being is 'asking us, as ministers, to go to a different place of listening'. Ian is right. Interwoven in this understanding is a portion of the *Basis of Union* that Ian loves. It is about 'awakening faith'.[5] Ian observes:

> There is something deeply respectful about our acknowledging that the Holy Spirit is doing something in peoples' lives – it's not about me telling you 'I've got something that

---

[5] 'Through human witness in word and action, and in the power of the Holy Spirit, Christ reaches out to command people's attention and awaken faith; he calls people into the fellowship of his sufferings, to be the disciples of a crucified Lord; in his own strange way Christ constitutes, rules and renews them as his Church.' *Basis of Union*, Paragraph 4.

you don't have it'. It is a different question; it's about 'you've got something that I resonate with as well, let's talk about it, let's try and be brave and try and explain what our experience of that is...'

Crying in the chapel

Liturgies for lament are a powerful way of giving space for salty tears to flow. Within the Uniting Church, there are written liturgies of sorrow that can be shared in worship, for example in the wake of disaster. There are prayers for the loss of a beloved child. There is a healing service for the breaking up of a relationship. All of these are optional, and they are a gift to the wider church. When we give space for collective grieving, with sensitivity and maturity, and without emotional manipulation, space for truth telling and healing is carved out. Within the service for the ending of a marriage, the following prayer is included. It begins with some of the words from the marriage liturgy and then gives space to name the agonising truth:

Marriage is a gift of God
and a means of grace.
It is founded on God's loving nature
and in the covenant of love made with us in Christ.

N and N entered into marriage with joy and hope,
affirming their trust in each other and in God
and pledging themselves to each other.

Yet through human frailty,
their love and companionship has become
brokenness and pain.

Others are affected,
especially the children and other members of the family;
friends have divided loyalties
and memories are spoiled.

We come to stand with N
as she/he grieves the loss of hopes and dreams
and faces the failure of her/his marriage/
in the ending of her/his marriage.[6]

After the prayers of letting go, and before laying on of hands, those gathered for this healing liturgy are invited to say:

N,
we share your sorrow,
we rejoice in your hope,
we pray for your new life.

    This is salty worship that seeks to be honest about the painful realities of life and to be open to the surprising healing of God in the midst of the mess.
    The invitation into weeping with those who weep is not a call into morbidity or dour community. Creating safe spaces for collective grieving is about claiming space for honesty.

---

[6] 'A service of Healing for Those Whose Marriage is Ending or has Ended' *Uniting in Worship 2* (Sydney: The Uniting Church Press, 2005), 549-556.

There is a desperate need for this right now. In our social media-driven culture, that constantly demands that people be happy, successful, #*living their best life* and posting about it on social media, creating space for shared tears and prayer is a profound and prophetic gift. This may indeed be one of the most lifegiving things we can offer as a church in our global village.

Salt water cleansing

When the tears can flow, it is often here that the healing can begin. This is because in letting the tears finally flow, especially with the solidarity of safe others, deep release can begin. Salty tears can enable something like a soul-cleansing. Curiously, the ways in which salty water can be cleansing are numerous. The good salty water of the ocean brings healing to many. In a far less organic setting, salty water cleanses in hospitals and medical clinics around the world, as saline water is utilised to tend wounds. Engaging with the idea of the church being a salt water community, a place where tears can flow and wounds be shown, where truth can be told and healing can begin, is a profound invitation.

Tears of laughter

We can, of course, cry when we are laughing very hard. This is an important point. This chapter has underscored the need to create space for tears in church if we are to be salty communities. However, it is no way being suggested that laughter has a lesser place. Laughter and practices of gratitude and expressing joy are also integral threads in the journey of being a disciple of Jesus and they form foundational components in our worship and our faith communities. Indeed, gorgeous resonances between Christian faith practices and discoveries in neuroscience are revealing what Christians – and our Jewish brothers and sisters – have intuitively known for centuries. When we articulate what we are grateful for, as a daily practice, when we notice and name moments of beauty and grace and goodness and give thanks for these, we will be more likely to notice these things each day and to experience increasing levels of joy and meaning in our lives.

Carving out space for the truth of sorrow, and making space for tears, does not discount the importance of praise, thanksgiving and practices of gratitude. Beyond the binaries that so often stifle the truth, we Christians are invited to hold the paradoxical truth of cross and resurrection, death and life, sorrow and happiness and, as Paul says, weeping and rejoicing. Underscoring the important place of salty tears in being church together does not displace the importance of laughter and celebration. As Ian wryly points out 'you also get sweaty when you dance!' Amen.

Wondering Questions

In your experience of church, have tears and grief been allowed or has there been an overriding pressure to be positive?

In your life, who has modelled that Christian faithfulness includes space for tears and sorrow?

How might you, and your church community, engage with creating spaces for lament?

Reflection and Prayer Resources

Light a candle.

Have a small bowl of salty water at the centre of your gathering.

Spend some time reflecting alone, or with your community, on the wondering questions.

Rest in some silence.

Sing or say the words of the hymn 'Brother Sister, Let me serve you' by Richard Gillard (650, Together in Song)

Close with the following prayer:

God of the tears, God of the cross,
God of the empty tomb and unexpected life,
help us to put down our shiny smiles
and allow ourselves to weep when the tears are banking up.

Help us also to make safe spaces for one another to weep
knowing that you weep with us
and knowing that your risen, healing life cannot be tethered.

Silence

You are invited to dip your finger in the salty water and make the sign of the cross on your own forehead and/or the forehead of one another, saying:

Christ of the tears and of the empty tomb be with me/you.

A blessing

To pray for yourself and for one another

May the protecting circle of the
Source of the elements,
Gentle Christ
and Holy Spirit,
be keeping us safe.

Chapter Four

Dark salty wombs

Our bodies course with salty water and our very beings grow up in good, dark salty wombs. What might this mean for how we understand ourselves as a salty church? Yet again, sacred Jewish and Christian texts offer us wisdom. In story after story, we hear about women who thought that they would never have children and who, yet, by the grace of God, miraculously give birth. Across these stories, longed for and unexpected babies grow up to be pivotal figures for God's people. Within sacred Jewish and Christian texts, these womb stories celebrate women and their faithfulness and the surprising new life that can grow when God and these women collaborate.

Within the Second Testament, in addition to significant miraculous birth stories, Jesus utilises the metaphor of the womb, of labour and of birth to speak of his own suffering and death, and the grief of the disciples, that will ultimately turn to joy in the resurrection (John 16:20-24).[7] Jesus also speaks about Holy Spirit birthing new life within the lives of followers (John 3:1-10). This theme of new birth within

---

[7] Paul also utilises the metaphor of labour and giving birth in Galatians 4:19.

Christian community is likewise taken up by the author of 1 Peter (1:3-7; 23 and 2:1-3).

Womb and birth imagery convey understandings of growth and new life. However, these metaphors are not enmeshed with assumptions that growth is connected to large numbers, grand buildings or established programs. Instead, the deep-down growing that occurs in the salty womb happens in secret and in kind darkness. What is more, this wondrous growth cannot be controlled, or even predicted, with any certitude. As any woman who has been unable to carry a baby, or who has lost, or nearly lost, a baby knows, womb growth is an entirely vulnerable affair. In reclaiming biblical understandings of womb imagery, as we think about being a growing and faithful church, we are offered refreshing insight.

Ancient mamas

In First and Second Testament texts that are largely written by men and addressed to men, there are notable accounts of women and their relationships with God. Before exploring some of these stories, it is important to underscore that these women focused accounts are still told from men's perspective. While this may lead some readers to dismiss these texts out of hand, it may yet be possible that insights can be gleaned if we read these sources with critical awareness.

Very early in the First Testament, we hear the primal story of Sarah (Sarai). This is a complicated tale. Readers are told Sarah, the matriarch of the people of Israel, endures years of agonising waiting for a child. In this biblical account, Sarah engineers a proxy heir by forcing her Egyptian slave woman, Hagar, to have sex with her husband Abraham (Abram). Hagar conceives and gives birth to Ishmael (Genesis 16:1-15). Ultimately, this does not bring joy to Sarah but, instead, Sarah is consumed with envy and fear (Genesis 16:4-6; 21:8-10). For Sarah, the idea of ever being able to conceive herself, becomes increasingly ludicrous. Like Abraham (Genesis 17.16-17), Sarah is described as laughing at the possibility of getting pregnant, even as God affirms this promise (Genesis 18:1-15). In this story, ultimately Sarah does conceive and goes on to give birth to Isaac. In this, her derisive laughter is transformed into mirth (Genesis 21:1-7). Isaac will grow to become a central figure in ancient Israel. However, this is not before Sarah again treats Hagar appallingly, instigating Hagar and her son Ishmael's banishment into the desert to die (Genesis 21.8-16). In this account, it is God who sees and intervenes to save and bless Hagar and Ishmael, amidst the violence perpetrated against them (Genesis 21:17-21).

In order to read this biblical account with honesty, the patriarchal context that shapes this story must be recognised. In this ancient society, women – free women and slave women – are both seen as lesser than men. Indeed, women are commonly construed as the property of men.[8] Within this context, producing children, particularly male children, is one

---

[8] This understanding is reflected in accounts of marriage in which women are 'given' by one group of men to another man. For example, Rebekah is 'given' by her brothers to Isaac in marriage (Genesis 24:1-67). The common understanding of women as property is bluntly spelled out in the Ten Commandments. Here men are called not to covet their neighbour's house, wife, slave, or donkey (in that order) or anything else that 'belongs' to their neighbour (Exodus 20:17).

of the only ways in which women are able to gain honour and 'redeem' themselves from the inherent worthlessness with which they are characterised by men.

This contextual reality does not excuse Sarah's behaviour as she seeks to create and protect male offspring. The often vile treatment of women in these accounts, both by men and by other women who profit from leveraging patriarchal assumptions to their own advantage, needs to be acknowledged and condemned. However, as we read, we need to understand the contextual realities that frame these narratives. In this ancient culture, in addition to the profound personal grief that a woman may experience if she is unable to conceive, the inability to have children could also be employed as a tool for societal shame and derision. This continues to be the case for women in many patriarchal societies today.

In another ancient biblical text, we see this reality writ large. In 1 Samuel, we meet Hannah. She is a person of faith who also longs for a baby but is unable to conceive. Within this account, shame is heaped upon Hannah by both men and women. Hannah is the one of the wives of Elkanah. While Elkanah's other wife Peninnah conceives and bears sons and daughters, Hannah is not able to have a baby. We are told that Peninnah makes life miserable for Hannah, as she taunts her for her childlessness (1 Samuel 1:1-8; similarly, Hagar derides Sarah in Genesis 16:4). Not only is Hannah harassed by Peninnah, the 'other' wife, Hannah is also misunderstood and derided by the religious elite. While Hannah earnestly prays for a baby, the priest Eli thinks she is drunk and condemns her for her 'inappropriate' behaviour (1 Samuel 1:9-18). Hannah's words to the priest (and to readers) are salutary:

> Do not regard your servant as a worthless woman, for I have been speaking out of my great anxiety and vexation all this time. (1 Samuel 1:16)

Despite the bullying and misunderstanding that Hannah endures, and despite the patriarchal assumptions that she is only a 'worthless woman', in this account God hears Hannah's prayers. Hannah becomes pregnant with a son, Samuel, who will grow up to be a great prophet. In response, Hannah sings a song of praise to God, the One who sees and values her. Hannah sings:

> Talk no more so very proudly,
>   let not arrogance come from your mouth;
> For the Lord is a God of knowledge,
>   and by him actions are weighed.
> The bows of the mighty are broken
>   but the feeble gird on strength...
> He raises up the poor from the dust;
>   He lifts the needy from the ash heap,
> to make them sit with princes
>   and inherit a seat of honour (1 Samuel 2:3-4; 8).

Here, in this song, the one who is perceived to be a 'worthless woman' according to patriarchal society, celebrates that God is the One who cares for those considered the least and who dismantles violent and excluding power structures.

Biblical marriage...?

Before attending to Second Testament examples of miraculous birth stories, I would like to invite us to pause to acknowledge these striking First Testament accounts of 'biblical marriage'. While in contemporary context, some people loudly claim that the Bible 'makes it plain' that marriage is between one man and one woman, this is clearly not the case. In stories such as Sarah's and Abraham's, sexual slavery is deployed. Furthermore, Abraham goes on to take another wife, Keturah and he also has multiple concubines (Genesis 25:1-6). Accounts of men like Elkanah having more than one wife abound. Perhaps most notable are the various accounts of the multiple wives, sexual slaves and sexual violence of King David. In 1 Chronicles 3, we hear that David has seven wives. In 2 Samuel 15:16, we discover that in addition to his many wives, David has ten concubines. In 2 Samuel 11:1-26, we read the distressing details of David's rape of Bathsheba and David's subsequent orchestration of the murder of her husband. It is abundantly clear that, in the Bible, marriage is not always between one man and one woman. As it turns out, biblical understandings of marriage are not so straightforward.

Women's business

Within the Gospels, which are grounded in First Testament accounts, we discover that the theme of surprising births and faithful women continues to be an important thread. In Luke's Gospel, we hear the story of Elizabeth and her husband, a priest, Zechariah (Luke 1:5-25). Like Sarah of old, we are told that Elizabeth is well past her childbearing years. Despite this perceived lack of 'blessing' from God, Elizabeth and her husband are faithful and righteous people who continue to love God. Like Hannah and Sarah before her, Elizabeth becomes pregnant through the gift of God's surprising grace. Elizabeth goes on to give birth to John the baptiser. In Luke's account, we are given a delightful glimpse of John, still enveloped in Elizabeth's good, dark, salty womb. Upon Mary's arrival at Elizabeth's house, the author tells us that Elizabeth feels John kicking about. Elizabeth, filled with Spirit Holy, understands that John is leaping for joy because of the presence of Jesus, enfolded in the nurturing space of Mary's womb (Luke 1:39-45).

The biblical theme of surprising births and God's unexpected action reaches something of a zenith in the story of Mary conceiving Jesus. Here Mary is not old and, as far as we know, Mary has not been afraid that she will not be able to have children. Mary is not even married (Luke 1:26-38). However, young as she is, Mary is asked to collaborate with the divine in the carrying of Emmanuel God-with-us (Matthew 1:23). For Mary to accept this invitation, in a patriarchal context in which unmarried mothers can be lawfully cast out of society or worse, this is clearly dangerous. Yet Mary chooses to say 'yes'.

While these ancient stories of women and babies and unexpected growth in salty wombs are informed by patriarchal assumptions, they are multidimensional, and may yet hold resources for us. In a culture in which it assumed that men are the central protagonists in politics, religion and life, in these accounts it is women who take centre stage. Even more, it is these women, and their good bodies, who are central in God's unfolding plans.

This theme explodes in technicolour in the story of Mary. According to the authors of both Matthew and Luke, the conception of Jesus has nothing to do with men, but instead, is exclusively women's business and it is sacred. This is no small issue. In these accounts of the birth of Jesus, we find God choosing to collaborate with one who is considered by society to be the least.

Here, patriarchal assumptions about power are upended and Mary realises this. Drawing from Hannah's theology and song (1 Samuel 2:1-10), Mary sings about the dreaming and energy of God that is dismantling the forces of the powerful and raising up the marginalised. Her praise includes this striking proclamation of God's reversal of human constructions of power that hinge on hierarchies, greed and domination:

> For he [God] has looked with favour on the
> lowliness of his servant...
> He has shown strength with his arm;
> he has scattered the proud in the thoughts of their hearts.
> He has brought down the powerful from their thrones,
> and lifted up the lowly;
> He has filled the hungry with good things
> and sent the rich away empty (Luke 1:48; 51-53)

That women and their salty wombs play such an integral role in the Christian story is striking. Perhaps because of the sentimentality of Christmas carols and the pristine perfection of nativity sets, we miss the raw shock of what is *actually* being claimed in these accounts. This was not the case in the early Jesus movement. Indeed, in the early church, such claims were a point of significant contention. In a society in which bodies, and in particular, women's bodies, were commonly construed as shameful, to claim that God, in Christ Jesus, dared to grow in such a space was barbaric to many.

Tertullian, who was born in the mid 100s C.E., was a highly educated Christian writer from Africa (current day Tunisia). His writing provides valuable insight into this period. Within his extensive work, and with a great deal of verbose rhetoric, Tertullian challenges a popular figure called Marcion. While Marcion was inspired by Paul and some aspects of the Gospels, Marcion was appalled by the claim that God would actually deign to take on flesh and become human in Jesus. According to Tertullian, it is the understanding that the Christ child would inhabit somewhere so 'unclean' as a woman's womb that was so utterly offensive to Marcion. Tertullian writes:

> Beginning then with that nativity you [Marcion] so strongly object to, orate, attack now, the nastiness of genital elements in the womb, the filthy curdling of moisture and blood, and of the flesh to be for nine months nourished on that same mire... Christ, there is no doubt of it, did care for the sort of person who was curdled in uncleannesses in the womb, who was brought forth through organs immodest, who took nourishment through organs of ridicule. (*Treatise on the Incarnation*, 4)

Scholars continue to debate whether Tertullian's own view of women, and their bodies, shares commonality with those he attributes to Marcion. I, for one, am looking forward to a conversation at the great feast. However, ultimately, after describing women's bodies in such offensive terms, Tertullian goes on to flip Marcion's world-view by arguing that this is exactly the place where God chooses to be vulnerable and take on flesh among us in the baby Jesus. For Tertullian, the reality that God chooses to be present as a vulnerable baby, in the womb, underscores the extraordinary breadth of God's love for humanity. He states:

> For God's [those born from the womb] he came down... If these are the constituents of those whom God has redeemed, who are you to make them a cause of shame to him who redeemed them, or to make them beneath his dignity, when he would not have redeemed them unless he loved them? (*Treatise on the Incarnation*, 4)

To claim that the Source of all would choose to contract to a span and grow – like us – as a baby in a woman's womb was utterly shocking in this patriarchal, and, often, misogynistic world. Knowing this, Tertullian does not seek to soften Christian convictions about the incarnation, but instead chooses to emphasise that God chooses to enter *this* very space, the depths of our frail humanity in the dark, salty womb.

Re-birth and the female divine

Within the Second Testament, alongside the womb stories of Elizabeth and Mary, the metaphor of birth and rebirth is important for understandings of the journey of discipleship. In John's Gospel, Jesus speaks of the need for followers to reborn, or born from above, through Spirit. Here the Johannine Jesus chooses to utilise womb imagery as he speaks of God's Spirit birthing followers into new life (John 3:1-10). It is women who give birth and here Jesus images Spirit giving people new birth. In this passage, Jesus chooses to utilise female divine imagery to speak of God and God's power. The author of John indicates that these words are shocking to Nicodemus, who misses the metaphor and talks about the absurdity of crawling back into his mother's womb. It is sad, but true, that female divine imagery continues to be shocking in the church today. This reality is reflected in the ways in which this imagery in the Bible is commonly downplayed or ignored.[9]

Spiritual birth imagery is not only a feature of John's Gospel. The author of 1 Peter also employs birth imagery to speak of the new life being experienced within Jesus communities. The author of 1 Peter states:

> Blessed be the God and Father of our Lord Jesus Christ! By his great mercy he has given us new birth into a living hope through the resurrection of Jesus Christ from the dead. (1 Peter 1:3)

The authorship of 1 Peter continues to be debated in biblical circles. Some argue that this letter is attributable to Peter, the loud-mouth disciple of Jesus. Others argue that this letter was likely authored by someone in Peter's circle. Still other scholars argue that this could not be the case and that the letter was written by an unknown, highly educated person who did not know the historical Jesus. What is more

---

[9] In the earliest church, Jesus is celebrated in the language and imagery of the female divine figure Woman Wisdom. For extended discussion of this evidence see my book: *Early Church Understandings of Jesus as the Female Divine: The Scandal of the Scandal of Particularity*, LNTS (London: Bloomsbury T&T Clark, 2016).

commonly agreed is that this letter is early. Indeed, it is possible that this letter was written before John's Gospel was penned. These shared references to birth imagery in both John and 1 Peter are intriguing.

The author of 1 Peter returns to the theme of birth later in this letter, claiming that people in the Jesus community are already experiencing this new life:

> You have been born anew, not of perishable but of imperishable seed, through the living and enduring word of God. (1 Peter 1:23)

While we cannot know with certainty whether John or 1 Peter was composed first, it is curious that both these Second Testament texts engage with female divine imagery to speak of the re-birth of followers. The author of 1 Peter goes on to invite Jesus communities to imagine themselves as hungry newborn babies who are nourished by Christ:

> Like newborn infants, long for the pure, spiritual milk, so that by it you may grow up into salvation – if indeed you have tasted that the Lord is good. (1 Peter 2:2-3)

Here, rather strikingly, the author encourages early church communities to imagine themselves breastfeeding from Christ.[10] This is an intimate invocation to be dependent upon Christ for our spiritual nourishment and growth.

---

[10] In contemporary biblical scholarship, this textual reality continues to be downplayed. This is despite the evidence that early church fathers such as Clement of Alexandria, writing in the 100s C.E., acknowledge and utilise this metaphor freely (see, for example, Clement of Alexandria, *Christ the Educator*, 41). For further discussion, see my book *Early Church Understandings*, 89-93, 183.

There is more at play in this metaphor. As anyone who has spent time with a hungry newborn baby knows, such little ones are not quiet or patient. Hungry newborn babies are demanding and disruptive, able to upend entire households within minutes and to sustain this disruption for hours. While commonly overlooked, the invitation to be like hungry newborn babies is, likewise, a call to become demanding towards, and dependent upon, Christ for our nourishment. The author of 1 Peter understands that the kind of growth that emerges from this authentic relationship with Christ is salvific, or to put this another way, it grows us up into healing and wholeness.

Considering patriarchal assumptions about the shamefulness of women and their bodies in the Common Era, as well as the value placed on honour, power and strength in the Graeco-Roman world, these celebrations of being re-birthed and becoming like hungry newborn babies are extraordinary. This is underscored by the reality that in this context children were commonly equated with weakness and being thought to be like a child was a source of embarrassment (Paul reflects this cultural assumption, e.g. 1 Corinthians 3:1-4). The counter-cultural affirmations of re-birth and the utilisation of female divine imagery found in places like John's Gospel and 1 Peter (and also in the Gospel of Thomas) may well be drawn from the remembered, and frankly shocking, teachings of Jesus.

In our own context, finally acknowledging and engaging with the female divine imagery that is present within the biblical text promises to enrich our understandings of being church and of our relationship with God in equally disruptive and lifegiving ways. I wonder how it might inform and transform our being church now, if we were to take seriously this call in 1 Peter? As church communities, how might it be to imagine ourselves like hungry newborn babies, loosening our desire for control, and becoming dependent upon Jesus and demanding towards him for our lifegiving growth and nourishment?

Salty womb churches

If churches were to take seriously the metaphor of salty wombs and the biblical call to re-birth, we may be changed. In order to take this birth imagery seriously, we first need to acknowledge the good, salty womb of Spirit who is the One who brings about this surprising new life. To engage with this womb imagery is also to be invited into a very different understanding of what a growing church might look like. Beyond certainty or strategic planning, womb-like growth, cultivated by Spirit, is an invitation into recognising the importance of the church becoming vulnerable.

Growth in womb spaces is not guaranteed. This growth cannot be controlled, and it largely happens in secret. To be a church that is open to the Spirit's rebirth and growth entails putting down our desire to be in charge of events or of the future. Instead, the call is to become focused on cultivating alertness to what Spirit is already growing within and among us and to join in.

Churches who engage with womb-like growth will no longer be fixated on the success of their programs or the numbers they hope to attract. Instead, alert to Spirit's prompting, such communities will be open to new ideas –

and sometimes strange ideas – without having set outcomes in mind. This model of growth is not dependent on human effort, but in contrast is reliant on Spirit's leading and growing up of the good. Inherent to this kind of growth is learning, as a people, to shut up and listen for Spirit's prompting. Like any pregnancy, this growth will be supported by various practices. Healthy eating might be likened to regularly attending to sacred text together. Resting and exercising well may be likened to continuing to cultivate practices of prayer and hospitality. However, just like carrying a baby to full term, even these practices do not guarantee 'success' for growth in the church. Engaging with the metaphor of being a salty womb like church invites us into an ongoing interior stance of vulnerability.

Rev. Sandy Brodine is one of the ministers within the Banyule Network in Melbourne. Within this network, people are exploring being church in many different ways. One of these expressions of church began with a disparate group of people meeting on a Saturday morning once a month for coffee and cake in a café run by the church. They called it TGIS – 'Thank God it's Saturday'. People gathered to talk about life, spirituality, faith and doubt. Many of these people had been burnt by the church, across various denominations. Among other things, this group of about eight to ten people began talking about their longings for what an authentic expression of church might look like. Sandy was part of these unfolding conversations. Instead of diving in with a solution, Sandy kept listening and asking questions.

As this gathering of people shared their disappointments and dreamings about church, one day Sandy asked, 'Well, if we were to worship, what would it look like?' Someone shared in response that it would be a 'space where we could belong'. In this, Sandy heard a name for this embryotic new expression of church. Over five years, the Space Community has continued to change and evolve. People decided to move from monthly gatherings to fortnightly gatherings and then to weekly gatherings. Engaging with Christian practices has been central for this group and various experiments have been made, some lasting and some quickly finishing. Contemplative practices continue to be integral. This is not a huge community – but the outgrowth in peoples' lives continues to be palpable.

Common Ground is another expression of church within the Banyule Network. This community meets on Sundays in a church hall. Worship follows the basic rhythm of the liturgy, but it is utterly fluid. Sermons do not take centre stage in this worship; instead, there is much conversation about the readings from sacred text. There are also spaces to engage with the biblical text in art and mess. These spaces for expression are not just for the children but for all. Someone might choose to go and do some journaling or sit in silent prayer, while others make art in response to the biblical readings.

Things are tried and put aside. There is lots of forgiveness in this community. Sometimes, halfway through worship, people will say, 'We don't like that song, Sandy. Let's sing this one instead'. And someone grabs their phone to put on a different song. Within Common Ground, there is growth in terms of faith, understanding and engagement with Christian practices. There is also growth in numbers, with this congregation having quadrupled in size. Their ever-increasing numbers, of mainly younger adults, means that they are now almost too big for the hall in which they gather.

However, there is more to say. Sandy highlights that for many this growth is hard to fathom. Sandy states:

> The expectation [can be] that new expressions of church are going to, somehow, bolt on and take on all of the edifice and try and prop that up.

For some people in more 'traditional' Sunday worshipping communities, because these new kinds of faith communities are not necessarily producing people to take up roles on the leadership team, join working bees to fix up the property, or sign up for the flower roster, these expressions of church are considered as 'not working' or 'not real church'. Here, we see cultural expectations of 'doing church' clashing with new (and perhaps ancient) ways of being a growing church in which buildings and cultural habits are not highly valued. Instead, these communities are focused on being disciples of Jesus. These kinds of growth are far more akin to the fragile growing that occurs within the womb, than they are to empire maintenance.

Another expression of womb-like growth in this Network is found in the Theology Hub. This group is made up of people from various backgrounds, from 30 years old to 80 years old who meet on a Thursday evening over a meal. They are studying together remotely at Pilgrim Theological College. Each semester, they do a unit together and Sandy serves as their tutor. As they eat together, they pore over their readings and wrestle with theology. Some stay on for the Space contemplative worship in the café afterwards. Some do not.

There has been all kinds of growth in this community. But this is not about numbers. The numbers have stayed largely the same, with around twelve people or so gathering each week. However, people are growing in their understandings of the biblical text, theology and what faith might be about. This is impacting on how people are living. Some in this group have gone on to take up new vocational roles in spiritual direction, chaplaincy and other settings. Spirit is at work birthing new life within and among them. But like the Common Ground community, this growth will likely not bolster the property fund or fill spaces on the grounds team. This is a far more vulnerable kind of growth, that comes without fixed outcomes.

Can we, as churches, put down our obsession with numbers and buildings and dare to be open to the deep down, interior growth that Spirit is yearning to birth in our lives and the lives of others? Are we open to allowing Spirit to grow new life within and among us? I wonder, can we forsake our desire to control outcomes, and even, potentially, lay aside some of our properties, so that we might have the time and energy as a church to focus on what is core – loving God with all our heart, soul and mind and loving our neighbours and loving ourselves (Matthew 22:34-40; Mark 12:28-31; Luke 10:25-28)?

Birth in the margins

As we discovered in the birth stories from the First and Second Testament discussed above, God is often at work in the margins, birthing new life in collaboration with those who are considered the least by society. This pattern is echoed throughout Jesus' whole ministry. Again and again in the Gospels we are told that Jesus chooses to go to the margins, feasting with and befriending those who are considered the nobodies and the failures (see Mark 2:13-17; Matthew 9:10-13; 11:19; Luke 5:27-32). As a church, I wonder if we are able to lay aside the desire to be in control and the desire to be significant? Can we put down our wistful longing to be powerful influencers, like (some of) our forebears from the Christendom church? How might it be to put the ego-driven agendas down and be prepared to meet Christ on the edges, just like we are called to do, in feeding the hungry, welcoming the stranger, clothing the naked and visiting the sick and those in prison (Matthew 25:31-46)?

Rev. Natalie Dixon-Monu is the minister at Boroondara Community Outreach in inner eastern Melbourne. This ministry is focused specifically with those on the edges. Often, participants are living with complex mental health issues and the challenges that can accompany such illness, including homelessness, poverty and extreme social isolation. Natalie loves this work on the edges. However, Natalie is clear that she is not taking Christ to the people here. In contrast, Natalie knows her work is about joining in with what God is already doing – and in the process – having God come to her in the people she ministers with.

Natalie tells the story of when she was a young candidate for ministry in her early 20s. At the end of her first year of ministry study, away from family and old friends, Natalie was homesick. Her mind was teeming with theology and with questions and she was feeling bamboozled, wondering why she hadn't been taught theology in church before and what ministry was really about. She was struggling. Amidst this, Natalie was sent on student placement to St Kilda Parish Mission, a centre that works with people experiencing homelessness and mental illness. Standing in the centre, her thoughts whirling, under her breath Natalie started to speak with God, saying:

> Where are you? Like, I don't even know where you are anymore and how the hell am I meant to be here, as a student minister on placement, somehow embodying your presence to these people when I don't even know if you exist anymore?... Do you exist? I don't know? Where the hell are you?

As Natalie was in the middle of having this conversation with God, a guy entered the centre and bounced up to Natalie. She immediately recognised signs of Schizophrenia in him. When Natalie greeted him, asking 'how are you?' He replied:

> Good, thanks. I have just seen Jesus.

Looking back now, Natalie reflects on her lack of experience at the time 'I must have given him a look, of "oh, somebody is probably not very well"'. In response, this man stopped and looked at Natalie and spoke with unnerving clarity and wisdom. He said to her:

> No, no, no, no. You look at the eyes of the people in this room and tell me you do not see Jesus.

Natalie says, 'I was told'.

I was told, 'You want to know where I am? I am right in the very people in front of your eyes'. That is the embodied Christ. From that day on, that has been my experience throughout my ministry.

To engage in being church on the margins is to recognise that God is already there. We do not take God in a box with us. We are not the heroes. Instead, with utter humility and openness, we are called to be tuned in to Christ's presence and to what Spirit is already birthing on the edges and to humbly join in.

This way of being demands that we put down our desire for control and for accolades. This also demands that we put down our longing for certainty, productivity or achievements, like 'fixing' people. Just as womb growth and birth are vulnerable and often beyond our control or our ken, so too is the good, deep-down growth and healing movement of God. Natalie reflects on this call for all Christians to be about the ordinary work of being present and kind (especially towards those who are considered the least) and to notice the presence of God right there in the midst of this caring. This may manifest in treating people who live on the street with compassion and integrity, remembering someone's name or how they like their coffee at a drop-in centre, doing the dishes for a community group, finding someone a jumper that fits better in an op-shop, tying someone's shoe laces if they can't reach down that far and, in Natalie's case, sometimes giving a person who is homeless a haircut. Natalie says:

> Those moments of serving – to me are the most profound moments. Because when I do that, I get that incredible sense of 'whatever you do to the least of these you do

unto me'. And I find in those moments of compassionate, little acts of kindness, the air becomes very thin, and the kingdom of God suddenly is within our midst... I get overwhelmed with a sense of here lies Christ.

Illustrating this womb-like growth that has nothing to do with control or fixed outcomes, Natalie shares a story from her time working in Juvenile Prison chaplaincy. A young teenage inmate had attempted to take his life and the prison staff were very worried about him. He wouldn't speak to anyone. He wasn't eating. They called Natalie to come in and see him. When Natalie arrived, she could see he was entirely shut down:

> I could see in his eyes... it was like he was already in the tomb – it was like death had its grip on him. There was a small fragile piece that was left there.

Natalie asked him if she could enter his cell. He shrugged. Natalie went in, but she didn't go in with a plan, a goal or a spiel. He was curled up on his bed in the foetal position. Natalie didn't speak or try and encourage him to share. Instead, she found herself cradling his head, stroking his hair and rubbing his back like a mother with a little child. And she found herself singing and humming a random lullaby. Inwardly, Natalie was praying and singing Taizé chants, with refrains like 'in our darkness there is no darkness with you, O God' echoing through her being. He began to weep and weep. Natalie wept too. At times, amidst the weeping, they shared in silence. They stayed like this for three hours with the singing, the tears and the silence. Natalie reflects that over this time:

It was like seeing someone being resuscitated. I could feel... his body was slowly warming up.

Years and years later, Natalie unexpectantly ran into this now six foot tall man at Centrelink, when she was there supporting someone else. His life was not 'fixed' or perfect (no one's life is). He was probably not a member of a church community. But when he saw Natalie, in the midst of the pain and injustice of trying to deal with bureaucratic systems, he immediately embraced her and their tears fell again. It turned out that he had no money because of a Centrelink administrative mistake. He was stuck in Victoria trying to get back home, interstate. That very morning, Natalie had been given some money by someone for the BCO program's work. She normally doesn't accept cash – but the person had insisted. The money was in her pocket, and she now offered it to this man. He was reluctant, but Natalie explained it wasn't her money to give – it was money for those with a need and he needed it to get home. Because of this gift, this man was able to catch the bus back home interstate.

Natalie doesn't know what the next chapter of this man's life held. It was most likely not easy, pain-free or 'solved'. Womb-like growth is not about fairy tale endings. Can we imagine being people of the way – salty womb people – who do not seek to control the outcomes and who may only journey with people briefly? Can we free ourselves up from our messiah complexes and project manager mindsets enough to let ourselves be open to Spirit's leading – just as we are right now – so that we can be present and compassionate, where we are called to be in this very moment?

It is interesting to note that Natalie is often asked by people from other church communities if she is exhausted or overwhelmed because she works with people on the edges of society. But this is not Natalie's experience. Speaking with emotion, Natalie says:

> I feel so blessed because I get to go and meet God every single day at work, and not only that, God blesses me.

Reflecting on this way of being church, collaborating with God in birth on the margins, Natalie states that the church's vocation is:

> Not to pretend to *do* church but rather to just *be*, and to be open to the mutuality of embodying God to each other. That is the moment of the profoundness. That is church.

In this *being* church, there is much energy and joy, as people join in with what God is already birthing. In Natalie's experience, the laughter flows in this work, as people are authentically open to one another – giving and receiving love – without an agenda to fix, or solve, or even recruit. As Natalie reflects:

> People are not asking to be fixed, they are just asking to be loved... The irony is that, in the loving, a whole lot of fixing happens... Because often what needs to be fixed is that they feel loved and embraced and worthy and that they get told that they are as much a child of God as anyone else.

Praying for new life

I wish to underscore one final feature of the salty womb metaphor. In the ancient story of Hannah and also, I suspect, in the life of Elizabeth, prayer plays a crucial role. I am struck by Hannah's utter honesty in prayer, as she bares her soul to God about her longing for a baby. I am equally struck by the embarrassment of the priest in the story who shames Hannah for her vulnerable praying. I wonder how often church congregations actually bring their (sometimes desperate) longings for new life to God in prayer? How often do ministers and congregational members pray for there to be new life birthed among, within and beyond their congregations? Further to this, I wonder how alert ministers and congregations are to the new life that God is already seeking to grow and, indeed, is growing in their midst and outside their doors? When we have set expectations about what growth and new life should look like, we can miss what Spirit is actually birthing right here, in front of us.

Wondering Questions

What challenges, or energises, you most about engaging with the Second Testament imagery of the Spirit giving us new birth and the call to be like hungry newborn babies who are nourished by Christ?

What challenges, or energises, you most about the idea that God's growth is 'salty womb growth' – and that the church is called into being vulnerable and open, instead of experts who control events or fix others?

How might you and your faith community cultivate openness to meeting Christ in the stranger and joining with Spirit on the margins where she is birthing new life?

Reflection and Prayer Resources

Ideally, share in this time in the evening as the darkness gathers. Keep the lighting low so that you can be in this kind dark space.

Light a candle.

Have an image of Mary and/or Elizabeth at the centre of your gathering.

Spend some time reflecting alone, or with your community, on the wondering questions.

Rest in some silence.

Read the story of Elizabeth and Mary meeting and enjoy the womb dancing within this account (Luke 1:39-45).

Conclude with the following prayer:

God of the good, dark, salty womb
we bring our longings to you for new life.
We delight in the new life you have already brought forth
in our community;
forgive us when we are too driven or despairing
to notice your new life before our eyes.

May we be open to your re-birth within and among us.
Help us to meet you in the margins
where you are already at work
and please embolden us to join in.

Silence

In the name of God, Holy One-Sacred Three:
Being of light, Bread of life, Birther of love
we pray. Amen.

Chapter Five

Salt that preserves

Salt is little. We shed salty tears. We grow in good, dark, salty wombs. Salt also preserves. In times before refrigeration – the vast majority of human history – salting food to keep it from going off was essential for survival. Evidence indicates that people from across cultures have been salting food stocks, in order to keep them edible over long winters and barren summers, for thousands of years. Preserving food products such as meat and fish in salt made it possible for them be traded across vast distances. Salt tubs were a common feature in homes in the ancient world. The importance of salt for the preservation of food, and thus the sustenance of whole communities, cannot be overstated.

Reflecting the importance of salt for survival in the ancient world, the etymology of the word 'salary' comes from the Latin *salarium*, originally meaning 'salt money', that was paid to Roman soldiers. Salting food in order to preserve it was, of course, the mainstream practice at the time of the writing of the Gospels. What might it mean for the church to be salt that preserves?

Origen was born in the 180s C.E., probably in Alexandria, Egypt. He was a gifted writer, a biblical scholar, a deep theological thinker and a mystic. Some accounts state that his own father was martyred for his Christian faith when Origen was still young. As Origen grew up, he too would face persecution, including imprisonment and torture, and he would die soon after release from a stay in prison. Origen faced harassment from within the church's growing hierarchy. It seems that church leaders were jealous of Origen's wisdom and popularity across Christian communities.

Origen wrote all kinds of texts including biblical commentaries and theological works. He also wrote a lengthy book, at the request of his friend Ambrosius, refuting the thoughts of someone called Celsus. Celsus had written a significant work, perhaps in response to Justin Martyr's writing, that aimed to disparage Christianity and to dissuade the educated classes from taking Christianity seriously. Within Origen's response to Celsus, he speaks of the church being salt. Here, Origen understands this metaphor directly in relation to salt's preserving qualities:

> For people of God are assuredly the salt of the earth: they preserve the order of the world; and society is held together as long as the salt is uncorrupted: for 'if the salt has lost its savour, it is neither fit for the land nor for the dunghill; but it shall be cast out and trodden under foot by people. The one that has ears, let them hear' the meaning of these words. (*Against Celsus*, Book VIII, chapter LXX)

For Origen, the deep down 'order of the world' is known in providential divine love which embraces 'all things' and is disclosed in person in Jesus Christ. Drawing from Philippians and Matthew's Gospel, Origen goes on:

... let the enemy come against us, and we will say to them, 'I can do all things, through Christ Jesus our Lord, who strengthens me'. For of 'two sparrows sold for a penny', as the scripture says, 'not one of them falls on the ground apart from your Father in heaven'. And so completely does the Divine Providence embrace all things, that not even the hairs of our heads fail be to be numbered by him. (*Against Celsus*, Book VIII, chapter LXX)

For Origen, it seems that Christians are salty preservers of the order of the world as they live (and die) in the self-same expansive love of the God of Jesus Christ.

How might we preserve the core?

Origen is surely right that preserving the centrality of divine love for all things is central. However, in contemporary context, the question of how exactly we are called to preserve divine love, as salty Christians, needs further unpacking. This is because Christianity's saltiness has been bleached out through compromises with Roman, and subsequent, empires for some 1700 years. The temptation to collapse into cultural answers, rather than theological responses, about what actually needs to be preserved – and how we are called to do this – is extreme. This is exemplified by the easy response that the church is here to preserve 'tradition'. If this is the answer to the question (and I doubt that it is), then we must ask whose tradition shall we preserve? How far back are we willing to go when we speak of preserving Christian traditions?

When some people speak of preserving tradition, they are referring to the church of their own childhood, in which pipe organs played or the Lord's Prayer was spoken in the language of 'thee' and 'thou'. In other contexts, preserving tradition might mean disallowing any musical accompaniment in worship at all, based on the view that earliest church communities sang unaccompanied (though we cannot know for sure how people sang and worshipped around tables in house churches in the first century). When we speak of salt that preserves, we need to guard against simply seeking to prop up our own preferences about how we like to do church and calling this the work of preservation.

Beyond debates about preserving worship styles, architecture or even lifestyle patterns, we get a sharp clue about preserving the core focus on divine love in the words of a young woman, Anna Harrison. I heard Anna speak at the Synod meeting of the Uniting Church a few years ago. Synod meetings occur every eighteen months in the Uniting Church in Victoria and Tasmania. In these five-day meetings, some three hundred people, lay and ordained members of the Uniting Church, gather from across these two states.

We seek to listen and discern together, pray and discuss together. We sit around large circular tables so that everyone can contribute to their table groups. We break out into working groups in order to hear yet more diverse voices. We do not rush to make decisions and decisions are not left in the hands of a few elite. Instead, we work hard together (some of these meeting days go well into the evening), with the conviction that we are all part of the priesthood of believers and that this is the most faithful way in which to lean into the movement of Spirit who moves where she will.

At this Synod meeting, Anna was asked to speak about the experiences of young people in the church and to respond to the question 'what are young people really seeking in church?' Anna began dryly, by stating that she was not the voice of all young people, and that young people were not a separate species. Then, in all seriousness, Anna said these words:

We want to know Jesus.

Her words cut to what is core, the heart of Christian convictions about divine love. Anna's words also resonated deeply with my own ongoing experiences of being in ministry. Slicing through preoccupations about what kind of music we might have in worship, or how we might attract the 'young people' while also preserving tradition, Anna spoke the truth. The one thing that we Christians have, and that other faith traditions, secular philosophies and lifestyle offerings do not have, are the wild heart convictions, stories, experiences, theologies, prayers, songs and practices of discipleship that all centre on the *person* of Jesus. This is the treasure at the heart of our faith. It is this, beyond everything else, that we need to preserve – our focus on divine love disclosed relationally in Jesus, if we dare to call ourselves Christians – *Christ* Ones.

In seeking to preserve the centrality of Jesus, at the core of our faith, I am not suggesting for a moment that this is bound up in simply reciting creeds or taking on ancient documents unquestioningly. Nor I am speaking about an exclusivist perspective that refuses to learn from other faith traditions or the insights of science, technology or philosophy. Rather, I am talking about cultivating communities in which the core work, the preserving work, is centered on coming back again and again to the person of Jesus – to the stories of Jesus in sacred text and to the possibility of authentic encounter with this One. I am talking about the kind of healthy faith communities in which all – ministers and lay people together – are encouraged to bring their questions, wrestle with the meanings of texts, engage in new and old theological debates and discern together about how life might be actually lived, day by day, if Jesus is in some way the face of God among us. Because this is the thing – if in some way Jesus is the God One, then everything changes.

If Jesus is Emmanuel God-with-us, then all images of God in which God is portrayed as the unpredictable overlord, the punishing old man on a cloud, the superhero who smashes enemies, all of these images need to be deconstructed in the light of Christ. If, as Second Testament texts proclaim in a myriad of ways, Jesus is infused with the 'fullness of God' (see, for example, the ancient hymn in Colossians 1:19), then all our images of God that do not look like Jesus need to be remade. For us as Christians, if Jesus is the Word made flesh, then how Jesus embodies power reveals how God embodies power. That is, in Jesus we encounter the rhythm of the universe and discover that it is kind and gentle. We discover that the Ground of our being flows in utter compassion, for friends and strangers, for failures and the lost, and even for the little birds.

In Jesus, we discover that God does not want to smash enemies but, shockingly, loves them, even to death, absorbing their violence rather than inflicting it. In Jesus, we witness radical divine generosity, in which healing, nourishing and stubbornly forgiving are all central attributes of God's being.

What is more, in all of this embodied, feisty compassion, Jesus keeps calling followers to join in, to collaborate in the inclusive, nurturing life and love of God. Taking this seriously challenges our understandings of power and of God. This also challenges how we are to understand what a life well lived might look like.

The scale of the deconstruction that is needed is immense. This is because it can suit us well to call ourselves Christians but to keep Jesus at a distance. It can be entirely convenient to claim the name of Christ and focus only on preserving, so called, Christian 'traditions' which are actually cultural accoutrements. It can be supremely useful to keep the Jesus of the Gospels at a distance and retain images of God as an iconic Zeus figure, who will smash (our) enemies and bless us with good things because we are in God's 'club'. By calling ourselves Christians, but keeping the stories of Jesus, the God One, tidied away, we can turn the God of Jesus Christ into just about anything.

When we choose to keep Jesus at a distance, safely tucked in greeting card images, Jesus can be made any colour (usually white) and our biggest backer as we choose to proclaim racism. This is despite the reality that Jesus is Middle Eastern, Brown and Jewish. We can choose to turn Jesus into a weapon of violence, for example claiming that the Christian God 'hates gays'. This is despite there being no record of Jesus making any comment about homosexuality in the Gospels and despite the reality that Jesus explicitly calls people not to judge others (see Matthew 7:1-5) and, instead, to be always about the work of loving all (see Matthew 5:43-48; 22:34-40).

If we keep Jesus at a distance, we can turn Christianity into a patriarchal religion in which only men are ordained or allowed to be leaders. This is despite the Gospels' repeated proclamations that Jesus affirms women in ways that shock the male disciples (see for example see John 4, and especially 4:27 for an amusing insight), and that Jesus chooses to appoint a woman, Mary Magdalene, to be the first apostle (see Mark 16:1-8; Matthew 28:1-10; Luke 24:1-12; John 20:1-18). This is also despite the Second Testament evidence that indicates that women are disciples. As well as the many named and unnamed women in the Gospels who follow Jesus and care for him (for example see Mark 15:40-41), Tabitha is explicitly called a disciple by the author of Luke/Acts (Acts 9:36). Women are also leaders in the earliest church. In Colossians, Nympha is greeted by name, along with the people of her house church (Colossians 4:15), and in Romans women are explicitly named as ministers and apostles. Here Paul includes an extended list of women leaders including Phoebe the minister and Junia the apostle (Romans 16:1-16).[11]

If we ignore the Gospels, we can convert the God of Jesus Christ into an ambassador for the free market economy with claims such as 'God helps those who help themselves'. This saying is not in the Bible and stands in direct contrast to accounts of Jesus who regularly helps those who are helpless

---

[11] Phoebe's role as a minister is often downplayed in translations. While Paul describes Junia as 'prominent among the apostles' (Romans 16:7), this reality was so shocking to later male church leaders that by the 13th Century Junia's name began to be changed in many biblical translations to a male name 'Junias'. This change was made in the attempt to eradicate evidence of this female apostle, despite the reality that there is no textual record of a male name form 'Junias' in any Greek and Latin speaking communities in the Common Era.

(see, for example Matthew 9:32-34; Mark 2:1-12; 5:1-20; 5:35-43; Luke 7:11-17; 13:10-17; John 9:1-34; 11:38-44). Tragically, with the Bible shut, we can also co-opt the radical way of Jesus into a tool for consumerist prosperity theology, with mantras such as 'God wants you to be rich' or 'God wants to bless you'. This is despite the reality that in the Gospels, Jesus repeatedly warns against the evils of wealth and calls people to live with extravagant generosity (see Matthew 6:19-21,24; 19:16-26; Mark 10:17-22; Luke 12:13-32; 18:18-25).

If we acknowledge that what is core to being church is Jesus, attending to sacred text becomes an essential and ongoing task. However, because of the way in which the biblical text has been misconstrued over recent centuries, I need to unpack what I am saying.

The way in which we approach the biblical text is crucial. The notion that the Bible is the literal 'word of God' is a relatively recent claim and, while it is popular in some circles, this is heresy. When Paul was writing angry and impassioned letters to communities in Galatia or Rome, he did not think he was writing 'the word of God'. The Bible is made of up diverse genres of writing including theology, prayer, gospels, letters (like Paul's) and dream journals. For us as Christians, all these texts point to the Word of God – Jesus. This is the unique thing about Christians – we do not have a book, or set of rules, at the core of our faith. Instead, we claim that we encounter God in Jesus. For us, Jesus is the Word enfleshed – God with skin on – the divine One who chooses to pitch tent with us in person (John 1:1-5; 14).[12]

---

[12] The *Basis of Union* is grounded in this understanding of Jesus as the Word of God and thus states that the Bible is 'unique prophetic and apostolic testimony, in which it hears the Word of God' (*Basis of Union*, para 5).

By regularly engaging with the disruptive and, frankly, shocking person of Jesus in the Gospels, in worship and in prayer, we can slowly be liberated from the fake gods that we construct and blasphemously dare to link with the name of Jesus. This is why, since earliest times in the Jesus movement, the pattern has been to come back to the biblical text week by week in worship and, together, focus our eyes again and again on Jesus. Coming to know Jesus is not a one-off event. It is a process, and it is the adventure of a lifetime. In affirming the central place of engaging with the biblical text, I am not talking about saccharine Bible studies in which set answers are expected for each question. I am not talking about taking the Bible literally. I am talking about taking the Bible seriously. This involves robust wrestling with sacred texts and exploring the ancient contexts in which these texts were written. This also involves actively engaging with insights from the wider scientific, artistic and intellectual world, as we continue to read sacred text together. The *Basis of Union* makes this plain:

> The Uniting Church acknowledges that God has never left the Church without faithful and scholarly interpreters of Scripture, or without those who have reflected deeply upon, and acted trustingly in obedience to, God's living Word. In particular the Uniting Church enters into the inheritance of literary, historical and scientific enquiry which has characterised recent centuries, and gives thanks for the knowledge of God's ways with humanity which are open to an informed faith. The Uniting Church lives within a world-wide fellowship of Churches in which it will learn to sharpen its understanding of the will and purpose of God by contact with contemporary thought. (*Basis of Union*, paragraph 11)

Creating opportunities for people, young and old alike, to actively engage with the wild person of Jesus is the core work that we need to preserve if we are to be salty Christians. Forget the battles about preserving, or discarding, traditions about pews or organs or particular hymn books. The central question is this – are we preserving the centrality of knowing divine love in Jesus? In our church, are people being given access to the Living Word, Holy Wisdom, and are they being given tools and permission to wrestle together with sacred texts and their meanings and how they might live right now *because* of who Jesus is in their lives?

Preserving the priority of tuning in

I would like to invite us to press a little harder into what it might mean to preserve the centrality of Jesus if we are to be a salty church. The desire to 'know Jesus', which Anna named, is not only about knowing in relation to intellectual discovery, bound up in acquiring knowledge or ideas about Jesus or about sacred texts. It is not even only about having clear theological rationales for how to apply these understandings in daily life. Christianity is, strangely, far more personal than this. To truly know someone is to spend time with them, to talk with them and listen to them, to be quiet with them together, to enjoy time with them and to be changed through this process of *being* together. If we are to be a salty church that is seeking to preserve the centrality of the divine love disclosed in Jesus, then assisting people to engage with how they might actually know Jesus in these *being* kinds of ways is core work. I am referring here to the sphere of the spiritual, or to put this another way, the world of prayer.

The word prayer is difficult to use these days. It has been hollowed out by piety, sentimentality and ignorance. Images of people praying in movies and in books are often characterised by a person either haggling with God for specific outcomes or grovelling on their knees with hands clasped in front of them. Across denominations, including the Uniting Church, churches have often created few spaces and little scaffolding for people to explore how they might actually *be with* Jesus in prayer. In order to know Jesus, in *being with* ways, there need to be spaces in church communities to engage with various prayer practices and to identify authentic prayer styles. We also need to create respectful room for wrestling with what the purpose of prayer might actually be and for discussing the reality that there can be seasons in life when prayer feel empty. While we might recite 'prayers' in worship and say to one another 'I will pray for you', so often we have not dived into, or shared, the treasure trove of spiritual resources that are available to us.

With only rudimentary prayer resources, perhaps taught in Sunday school, this can leave people starving. Prayer that is understood to be about reciting particular words or listing the things we are worried about in a 'shopping list of doom', are unlikely to support us in the long dark night of the soul, or in the shadow of the valley of death, or in dealing with a messy divorce, unexpected unemployment, struggles with mental health or during a global pandemic. When tragedy happens in life and people are left spiritually malnourished by the church, they often choose to walk away in order to explore 'alternate' spiritual options. Or they decide to walk away from the soul-side of their lives completely.

The tragic irony is that there is a multiplicity of nourishing spiritual practices within Christian tradition that are meaningful and focus on helping us to *tune in* to the vibrations of divine love. In engaging with such practices, and learning to tune in, we can begin to meet Jesus as we are, not as we think we should be. Contemplative prayer traditions have much to offer us in this sphere. Some of these traditions go back to the very early church, some can be traced to practices of the desert mothers and fathers, while others are from more recent centuries. These spiritual ways of *tuning in* to God include prayer practices such as *Lectio Divina*, or Sacred Reading, prayer walking (or prayer weaving), engaging with a prayer word or phrase from a Psalm, journaling, singing and praying in silence.

Within the Banyule Network, Rev. Sandy Brodine shares a story of offering different prayer practices. When COVID-19 lockdown hit, a small group of people all aged over 70 were already exploring Christian practices week by week. This group suddenly had to move their weekly gatherings online. Sandy had been planning to offer an introduction to breath prayer, in which people are invited to quietly sink into the rhythm of their breath, perhaps imagining Spirit filling them as they breath in and filling the space as they breath out. However, with lockdown rules now in place Sandy explained to everyone, via their computer screens, that breath prayer wasn't going to work online. She advised the group that she would give them the techniques to try at home in their own time and that they could reconvene the following week, to talk about their experiences of engaging with this practice. The people's response? They said:

> No! We are going to do it now.

Sandy listened and said:

> Alright then, this isn't going to work, but ok, if you want to, that is fine.

So, with everyone in their own homes, joining via computer screens in the first week of lockdown, Sandy led them in breath prayer. They spent five minutes sinking into this contemplative tuning in together. In the silence, people could hear the bird song in one another's gardens, as they were each cocooned separately in their own homes. When this shared time of praying in silence was over, Sandy asked 'How was that for you?' She then looked up at her screen, at everyone's faces. She describes what she saw like this:

> You know that beatific smile people get when they have, kind of, been engaged with God? They all sat there looking at me like that... and it was just this moment of 'ahhh'.

Amen for moments of 'ahhh' and the core work of carving out spaces for people to actually encounter the Source of all in the middle of ordinary life (even across computer screens). Another prayer style that is a treasure to share with people is Imaginative Composition, a type of praying that is detailed in the work of St Ignatius of Loyola. In this prayer style, we are invited not just to study the Bible intellectually, but to allow our deepest longings and imaginings to emerge and to be open to encountering Spirit within this praying. A particular Gospel passage is chosen. It might be an account of the last supper, or the feeding of the multitudes, or a healing story. Then, in silence, we allow ourselves to imagine being in the scene. Supporting questions are asked as people sink into the stillness. These questions might include: What do you hear? What do you see? What do you smell? How are people reacting to Jesus? What do you do?

This prayer practice is not about getting 'the right answer' to a text, or 'solving' it. Instead, this practice is about allowing our whole being to be open to God, including our imagination and senses. This type of prayer practice gives space for those tucked away parts of ourselves that we may be too shy or ashamed of to acknowledge, to finally emerge and for Spirit Holy to meet us there with her cleansing, healing presence. I remember once offering this prayer style within a worship service in a little rural church in a paddock. It was close to dusk and it was on the cusp of Christmas. Instead of loud carol services, or fast paced events, together we gathered in a circle to hear, and enter, the nativity account from Luke. At the centre of this quiet worship space was an empty Coolamon, a symbol of waiting for the Christ child, to be birthed in our midst.

During lockdown at Richmond Uniting, we have begun meeting over livestream for Midday Prayers each week. This space utilises the same, simple, inclusive liturgy each Wednesday. Within this thirty minute service, there are big chunks of silence together. Like the group Sandy describes, we also hear the birds singing – and the chooks chortling – from house to house, across our screens. Time expands in this shared space and sometimes the sense of God's presence, pulsating between us, strikes me deeply. In this quiet service, we hear the Psalm and the Gospel reading for the week, but there is no explication or discussion. This is a shared resting time in God. There are spaces for people to name their prayers of gratitude and to pray for those who are on their hearts. Each week, we conclude with the Lord's prayer and a blessing for one another. It is a sacred pause in the middle of the week and this rhythm of prayer connects us with far older Christian traditions.

Within the *Didache*, an early church document thought to date from around the end of the first century, we find a series of simple instructions about how to be church together. Among these is the instruction to pray the Lord's Prayer often:

> Nor should you pray like the hypocrites, but as the Lord commanded in his gospel, you should pray as follows: 'Our Father in heaven, may your name be held holy; may your kingdom come, may your will be done on earth as in heaven. Give us today our daily bread. And forgive us our debt, as we forgive our debtors. And do not bring us into temptation but deliver us from the Evil One. For the power, the glory are yours forever'. Pray like this three times a day. (*Didache* 8:2-3)

In this context, in which the Roman empire was the kingdom and Emperors, not uncommonly, claimed to be divine, Jesus communities are urged to engage repeatedly – each day – in a prayer that celebrates, and seeks, the growing presence of an alternate, unseen kingdom. This is both a practice of payer and an act of rebellion.

While our culture deeply values spontaneity, my suspicion is that there is deep wisdom embedded in this instruction of the *Didache* to pray the Lord's prayer three times a day (likely once in the morning, at midday and in the evening). Creating simple rhythms like this each day, to stop, be present to God and realign with God's dreamings, has the potential to carve out space for us to come to know the divine love of Jesus more deeply and for us to actually experience transformation in our lives.

This is particularly the case in contemporary culture, in which our time and attention are continuously dominated by work, seduced by busyness and assaulted by the addictive pull of social media. By establishing simple and regular daily rhythms to stop and to shut up and to be open to the divine other, we may be able to reclaim our time and attention. In cultivating sacred pauses and allowing such practices to grow muscle strength in our lives, we may be able to be present more naturally to ourselves and our environment, to God and to others, and to what is actually most important. As it turns out, it may well be that this ancient call within the *Didache* to pray the Lord's prayer three times a day, is still a call to prayerful and rebellious action.

Rev. Salesi Faupula is the minister at Canterbury Uniting Church in the inner east in Melbourne. This is a largely Tongan congregation, and it is a growing congregation. I have heard from others that this faith community is almost too big for its current buildings because of its ever-increasing numbers. Salesi did not tell me this. When I ask Salesi about the congregation, he points to a different type of growth. Salesi shares that they currently have six people engaged in a Period of Discernment, the Uniting Church process, that is open to all, that creates space to intentionally explore God's dreamings for your life with a mentor and with others.

Within this thriving congregation, there are various groups, including womens groups, mens groups, family groups and the youth group. Salesi talks about how these groups have continued to evolve through listening as a congregation for new ideas. This has brought changes to this growing congregation. Instead of the more traditional cultural hierarchical model of only elders being the ones who are able to speak in certain gatherings, this congregation is now creating space for all voices to contribute. This is a departure from past patterns of being church and is inviting deeper vulnerability. Now, because of these changes, younger members of the congregation, both young men and young women, are sharing their gifts and insights and taking up leadership roles. Amidst these changes, Salesi talks about the integral focus across these groups:

> It is about inspiring one another, growing, and building up one another in faith... The centrality of Jesus is key to the way in which we do things.

Salesi describes the youth group which is made up of young people of various ages, from their first year of high school, right up to those who are young adults. Like youth group back when I was a teenager, this youth group meets on Friday nights. However, this youth group is not simply focused on games or scavenger hunts. While fun activities form a part of this youth group, this is not at the core. As Salesi says:

> I think there is a sense that what will hold us, and what will ground us, will be that sense of how we relate to Christ... and scripture is the pointer.

Salesi explains that this space to engage meaningfully with Christ and with sacred text within the youth group community is dynamic and interactive:

> It is highly relational... and about exploring who Jesus is for them... It is not exegetical as such, it is more drawing on experience and then, also, trying to engage with some of the current issues we are going through.

This time of wrestling with the Bible is led by Salesi or one of the youth leaders. However, cultivating interactive dialogue within this youth group Bible study has taken time. This is because the young people were used to a far more 'ritualistic' way of doing Bible study. Salesi describes how, in the beginning, young people would come in with Bibles, but that they were on a kind of 'auto-mode'. He realised that they 'switched off' and 'whether we did this or not didn't really make any difference'. So the leadership team began exploring doing Bible study very differently, focusing on what was happening in the world and for young people at school and in their own relationships. Salesi began challenging them with the question:

How do we take the Bible seriously?

Salesi reflects on the impact of asking this particular question:

That was a shocking question, I think, at first. It did rattle them a little bit... we have moved it way from... this book that no one questions... to a point where we could actually ask questions and be ok with this... They had a lot of questions, but they didn't think they could ask them in that particular context, until now. We now say to each other 'questions are ok and questions are important'... There has been a sense of honesty in the way in which we have been trying to express ourselves and engage with one another. And I think this has been a real, real blessing for us.

Through creating this authentic space for questions and wrestling, the community is growing in trust and spiritual depth and Salesi has noticed that the 'quieter' voices are now offering their deep wisdom into the group.

As well as taking the Bible seriously, the youth group has also begun exploring how they can engage in mission. Instead of this youth group being insular, self-serving or focused on being a social club for entertainment, the gifts that these young people bring, and Jesus' call to serve those in need, are being taken seriously by this congregation. As a consequence, the youth group has now engaged with mental health training and they have started getting involved in serving in a local soup kitchen.

In our social media-saturated world, young people are constantly being marketed to. They are bombarded with messages about how to look and how to act. They are endlessly fed the lie that their value is dependent on how many 'likes' they have or how beautiful or popular they are. The notion of serving others is far removed from the meaning offered by consumer culture. Amidst this assault on the very beings of young people, what a gift this youth group is offering. Here, young people are being given space to be themselves, in a setting in which they are truly valued and cared for. This congregation has built a counter-cultural space for young people to safely voice their deepest wonderings about life, meaning, the universe and everything. These young people are being taken seriously as they take the Bible seriously together and they are being given opportunities to make a meaningful difference in the lives of others as they live out their faith.

In this setting, week by week, this congregation is together preserving what is core. They are carving out space for young people and older people to authentically know Jesus – the One who discloses the divine love at the heart of the universe. Furthermore, in an ongoing way, this church community is daring to wrestle together with what it means to be followers of Jesus in daily life. I wonder how churches across this land might flourish if we sought to preserve the centrality of this work?

Wondering Questions

How do you respond to the claim that knowing Jesus is the core to preserve?

How much time and energy does your faith community spend creating authentic space for people to get to know Jesus more deeply, in theological wrestling and in spiritual practices?

What new things might you do (as a community or as an individual) to make this a priority?

Reflection and Prayer Resources

Light a candle.

Gather some little dishes of salty preserved foods, e.g. olives, pickles, etc.

Place these at centre of your gathering.

Spend some time reflecting alone, or with your community, on the wondering questions.

Rest in some silence.

Share in your salty feast and some conversation about the most meaningful times in which you have come to know Jesus more deeply in church settings.

Conclude with the following prayer:

Jesus, the hospitality of God,
we praise you for gathering us into the feast of your love.
For the ways in which the church has preserved your love at the centre, we give thanks.

silence

For the times in which we have preserved human traditions and agendas instead of focusing on your presence and compassion, we seek your release.

silence

Please draw us back to you and help us to cultivate communities in which people may discover your embracing love for all things.
Amen.

Chapter Six

Salt as seasoning

It is time to confess. I am not a sweet tooth. I have never liked lollies. I could take or leave cake. But salt is a different matter altogether. I love savoury food and salty snacks. Salt is a mysterious substance. It is not quite a spice and not quite a herb, but it is able to draw out the good flavour of so many other foods. How might we understand Jesus' metaphor of being a salty church in relation to the seasoning quality of salt? In the Second Testament text of Colossians, the author ponders this very question. Whether the author of this letter is Paul, or perhaps Timothy writing with Paul, or someone else writing in Paul's name, we do not know. Biblical scholars continue to debate the authorship of the letter. However, here, perhaps drawing from traditions about Jesus calling followers the 'salt of the earth', the author encourages this early Jesus community to live out their faith in the following way:

> Conduct yourselves wisely towards outsiders, making the most of your time. Let your speech always be gracious, seasoned with salt, so that you may know how you ought to answer everyone. (Colossians 4:5-6)

Here, the Jesus community is told to be conscious of how they come across to those who are not followers of Jesus.

They are explicitly called to *always* speak graciously, as they go about their daily business in the wider community. Here, the ideas of speaking graciously and speech that is seasoned with salt are linked together.

I wonder what the world might be like if Christians took this call seriously. Imagine if people who are part of the church, across denominations, were shaped by the call to *always* speak graciously with people who are not part of the church. To take the call of Colossians seriously is to be invited into a worldview in which our daily actions, including even our passing interactions, all matter. Each conversation that we have becomes a place where we can, and ought to, sprinkle grace. That is, if we Christians know the love of Jesus, the God One, within our lives, we should let this shake out of us each time we speak. By doing so, the author seems to suggest, we will be seasoning our communities, drawing out the good, the tastiest flavours, for everyone.

What might it mean for how we live, if we understand that a core aspect of discipleship is to be salty seasoners of conversation? How might it be to imagine that it is sacred work to sprinkle graciousness wherever we go? As we think about our relationships and connections within the world beyond the church, this is a creative invitation and a profound challenge. If we take this invitation seriously, we will need to become more aware of how we communicate with others.

We will be forced to ask questions of ourselves. Are our interactions with those beyond the church (as well as those in the church) peppered by gracious speech, or are we known for our gossiping? Are we seasoning our conversations (whether face to face or on social media) with the humble compassion of Jesus or are we habitually focused on virtue signaling, character assassination or competing? When we are in conversation with others who are rude about someone else, do we choose to sprinkle a disruptive gracious word, reminding people of the dignity of each person and the call to love enemy, or do we remain silent for the sake of keeping the (false) peace? Is our speech gracious, open and hopeful, infused with the presence of Spirit, or we are gloomy or sarcastic? Do our interactions enhance the qualities – the flavours – of compassion and kindness in our world or do our words leave a bad taste?

In order to be honest with ourselves about how we communicate, we may need to stand back a little, and internally observe our interactions with others. We may also need to do the very brave thing and ask for feedback from people we trust, like a Spiritual Director or mentor or friend. Cultivating a prayer practice that has chunks of silence can also be a way (it is often painful) for Spirit to alert us to the shadow sides in our lives, including our habits of speaking in ugly or toxic ways.

A crucial aspect about the seasoning quality of salt is volume. It is possible, even I admit, to over salt food and to spoil the taste of a meal. Just as too much salt ruins the taste of everything else, too much speaking can also be destructive. The invocation to always speak graciously, seasoning conversations with a salty presence, is not a call to be constantly talking about our religious convictions. Nor is this a call to be constantly talking. Just as with the seasoning of salt, in which a little goes a long way, we are called to be seasoners of conversations. And, as the author of Colossians makes plain, when we do choose to speak, we need to be kind in our well-chosen sprinkling of words. In our current context, in which Christians have caused significant amounts of pain and trauma to people, by dumping religious views upon them like giant salt kegs of judgment, hatred and fear, this is crucial to underscore.

Churches with seasoning words

How might we – as church communities – collectively model speaking sparingly and graciously to those who are not Christians? Rev. Rachel Kronberger is the minister at Pilgrim Uniting Church, Yarraville, in the inner west of Melbourne. This church is embedded in the local community, with most people who attend living locally. The congregation runs an op shop, a play group operates from the church site and the faith community is well known for sharing hospitality in this urban 'village'. In recent years, at various points, the congregation has created gentle little 'speech bubbles' with the wider community. One of these examples was creating a 'peace tree' in the wake of an event of tragic violence in the world. A little plastic bag of coloured ribbons was stuck to the church letterbox at the front of the church, together with a notice inviting people passing by to tie a ribbon onto the tree if they would also like to pray for peace. In the first afternoon the bag of ribbons was empty and the tree in the church garden was covered with ribbons-prayers. Over several days more and more ribbons were tied to the tree as quiet prayers continued to be offered. Children passing the church on the way home from school loved joining in and so

Salt as seasoning

did older people. This little salty offering of a church speaking graciously (with very few words) communicated a great deal. For some in the broader community, Pilgrim Uniting is now known as the 'peace tree' church.

Rachel reflects that communicating in such ways as a church challenges us to remember that we are not the 'meat', the substance, instead we are called to be spicy seasoners in the world. Rachel says:

> We are here to be the salt. So it is about, you know, looking for where the substance is, where we are, and looking at how we can make it something delicious, something beautiful where the sweetness can emerge.

The 'peace tree' is a perfect illustration of this kind of salty presence in the wider community. This is because the invitation to pray for peace was based on the assumption that the 'meat', the substance, was already there. The church trusted that people in the wider community were already longing for peace and for ways to connect with the divine. Pilgrim Uniting simply drew out this taste, by offering a way to give creative expression to this longing.

A few years ago, the congregation chose to replace an unused wooden church door, that faced the street, with a glass panel. This has created a permanent window space that has become an interface between the congregation and the wider community. In each of the church seasons, a new tableau is placed in this window. For Palm Sunday, there may be palm leaves filling this space, accompanied by a poster about the upcoming Refugee Rally. In Advent, week by week, the themes of hope, peace, joy and love are explored. At Christmas a nativity scene is placed in this window.

This space is quite intentionally not word heavy. In a little frame, a few verses of sacred text that gives context to the tableau, nestles on the floor of the scene. By choosing to rely on images and using only a sprinkling of words, this little window space is creating gracious salty space for deeper connection. Not only do people stop to look at this changing window scene, Rachel also shares that some local people who are not members of the congregation now come to pray at this window.

At Richmond Uniting, several years ago, the congregation decided it wanted to communicate more clearly and lovingly with the wider community. A huge printed banner now stretches along the fence, with the words: 'Church – but not as you know it'. Accompanying these words is an image of a needle with all kinds of coloured strands, threading through the eye. Multiple people who attend Richmond Uniting have told us that they were first drawn to the congregation because of this banner. At Fairfield Uniting, a beautiful garden has been made at the front of the church and the very steps are painted in rainbow colours communicating, without words, an inclusive welcome for all. As congregations, when we think about how we might speak with the wider world and sprinkle a word of grace, thinking about the 'vibe' of our buildings, what messages our buildings and signs are actually communicating, is of critical importance.

In our technological age, there is another aspect of communication that is vital for the church to consider when it reflects on speech that seasons. These days, when people are deciding whether to attend a church or not, it is likely that they will first visit a congregation's website, or check out its social media presence, to find out more. If a church website is two months (or two years) out of a date, or is ugly, or is filled with information about the history of the building rather than what the community actually believes about the divine who comes to us in Jesus, people are unlikely to engage further. An up-to-date and eye-catching website is an essential medium for gracious, salty speech and deserves to be a core priority in church budgets *if* a congregation is serious about sharing the good tidings of Jesus.

On a website, faith communities are given the rare opportunity to speak in their own words and images about the wild way of Jesus to the broader community. When church websites communicate an authentic word of hope about what they actually believe and how this is leading them to worship and to live differently, they offer a spicy invitation to all to come and see.

Let's talk about...

The call for Christians to speak graciously is not just about churches communicating kindly to the wider community. This call in Colossians is also a challenge to each one of us, individually, to find ways to speak in authentic and kind ways about our faith. However, the fear of saying the wrong thing, or being offensive, or being like 'those Bible-bashing' Christians, leads many Christians to say nothing. While sharing sympathy with this view, this is not a faithful response. The imagery of salt is profoundly helpful for us in this context. Speaking about our faith to those without a church connection is about sprinkling a word here and there, so that people may catch a taste of the good news. In doing so, people may then choose to ask us more about this strange hope and love that infuses our lives, and opportunities for deeper conversation may arise. It is in the context of building authentic, caring and respectful relationships that this kind of sharing becomes possible.

Sometimes the beginning of sprinkling gracious words can simply be in letting people know you go to church – so that the door is left open for questions. Sometimes this might be in offering to pray for someone, or to light a candle for them. This sharing of a few kind words might be reflected in sending someone a blessing, or word of hope, or a poem in a card or email. When conversations about faith do open up, at least initially, sharing personal experiences and stories, will communicate far more deeply than attempting to summarise a whole theological position. However, this can feel profoundly intimidating in our culture which shies away from talking about religious experience – even in the church.

Recognising this challenge, at Richmond Uniting, at various times, I have invited us to practise putting gracious and authentic words around our faith, within the context of worship. For example, I have asked people to share in small groups their responses to questions such as 'what drew you to being a Christian?' And 'how is your life different because of Jesus?'. On one such occasion, a person who was an asylum seeker shared his own experiences with the rest of the congregation. He explained, in worship, that while in detention on Christmas Island, he noticed that the Christian asylum seekers had an inner peace, despite being in detention.

He was amazed by this peace that they exuded, especially in such difficult circumstances. It was this that drew him to find out more about Christianity.

In our current cultural context in which all kinds of dreary stereotypes about Christians hold sway, debunking some of the cultural scripts about Christianity will likely be necessary before any meaningful conversation can begin. People can make all kinds of assumptions when they find out you are a Christian. These views are often constructed out of media representations and are usually pretty far off the mark. People have apologised to me for swearing, assumed that I believe the world was made in six days, that I am anti-science, or that I must condemn gay people, when they have discovered that I am a Christian. Part of sprinkling conversations with gracious words in our post-Christendom era, is creatively and kindly debunking the ludicrous images of Christianity that people often assume to be true.

Salted with fire be at peace with one another

In Mark 9, we hear about an argument between Jesus' male disciples. They have been disputing among themselves which one of them is the most important (Mark 9:33-34). The author of Mark makes it clear that they really haven't been listening to Jesus' words for some time. In Mark 8 and 9, Jesus repeatedly talks about the reality that divine power looks very different to human power. Jesus says he is going to be betrayed and violently killed and, what is more, Jesus says that to be a follower of Jesus means entering into this way of humble, non-retaliation and self-giving (Mark 8:31-38; 9:30-32, see also 10:32-34).

In this Gospel, Jesus knows they have been fighting and when they are in the privacy of the house Jesus challenges them, asking them about the nature of their conflict. We are told that Jesus responds to their power plays by drawing their attention to a child. Jesus brings this child to the centre, a little one, considered entirely unimportant in the patriarchal and hierarchical worldview of the Common Era. Jesus then goes on to proclaim the unthinkable:

> Whoever welcomes one such child in my name welcomes me, and whoever welcomes me welcomes not only me but the one who sent me (Mark 9:37).

Here, Jesus is effectively saying, 'Look, the one you think of as the least important, is where you will find me and where you will find God. Get your heads checked'.

In unforgettable language, Jesus then makes clear that the 'little ones' must be safeguarded in Christian community and that there will be severe consequences for those who hurt them (Mark 9:42-48). These graphic words give me hope. Here it is proclaimed that those who think they can hurt children, or vulnerable people, and get away with it, will be exposed and will, ultimately, face costly consequences.

After this proclamation, in Mark's Gospel, Jesus then goes on to speak about about salt and seasoning. Jesus states:

> For everyone will be salted with fire. Salt is good; but if salt has lost its saltiness, how can you season it? Have salt in yourselves, and be at peace with one another. (Mark 9:49-50)

In response to the male disciples jostling for status and privilege, Jesus does not seek to sooth their insecurities but instead, disrupts their understandings of power. Jesus calls them to see God's presence and power in the place they least expect it, with those considered the least important in society. Jesus then goes on to affirm the centrality of honouring the little ones and being at peace with one another. It is here that living in peace is linked with saltiness.

Within this passage there is a reference to being 'salted with fire'. This language is curious to say the least and leaves biblical scholars perplexed. In our own context, trying to understand a connection between salt and fire can be difficult. However, it is likely that for first readers of Mark, living in the Common Era, the links between salt and fire were more obvious. In Jewish sacred text, instructions are laid out for the practice of salting food offerings that are then burned. Within the First Testament text of Leviticus, as instructions are given about how to make grain offerings of first fruits, the text states:

> You shall not omit from your grain offerings the salt of the covenant with your God; with all your offerings you shall offer salt. If you bring a grain offering of first fruits to the Lord, you shall bring as the grain offering of your first fruits coarse new grain from fresh ears, parched with fire. (Leviticus 2:13-14)

Here salt and fire are explicitly linked together in the practice of making cultic thanksgiving offerings to God (see also Exodus 30:35; Ezekiel 43:24).

It is likely that in Mark, as Jesus speaks about salt and fire, this kind of cultic practice informs this imagery. This is underscored by the reality that in some early manuscripts the additional words 'every sacrifice will be salted with salt' are included. It may be that here cultic thanksgiving practices are being expanded, or reimagined, so that the very lives of followers are called to be salty offerings to God. Similar ideas about becoming a living sacrifice are taken up in other early Jesus communities (for example, see Hebrews 13:15-16). In Mark, this salty-living-offering imagery is linked, in particular, with being at peace in Christian community.

When we keep in mind the context of this whole passage in which the disciples have been jostling about power and Jesus gives stark warnings to those who misuse their power (Mark 9:33-48), we discover a piercing challenge. Here, the gathering together of imagery of being 'salted with fire', ideas of sacrifice and the challenge to living peaceably together, may reflect ideas about being purified and refined for peace. That is, in the process of allowing our lives to become a salty offering, no longer driven by power plays, but instead focused upon honouring and protecting others, especially the 'little ones', our ego-driven agendas are burned away. Like the fighting disciples, this will be a costly process of having our assumptions about power deconstructed, so that we may actually be able to embody God's peace together. In being thus salted and refined, our lives might begin to offer a taste of the kingdom, a sample of God's dreaming.

To take this Markan understanding seriously is to reimagine dominant constructions of church. When Jesus communities embody structures in which the last are first and the 'little ones' (including children and vulnerable adults) are honoured, safe and included, we become a salty, seasoning gift, sprinkled across our global village. When Christians live in authentic peace, no longer sniping, competing or lording it over one another, we offer a spicy alternative to the dominant models of power in our global village that are commonly shaped by coercion, fear, exclusion and violence. And when we embody Jesus' radical hospitality, raising up those considered unimportant, we draw out the good, offering a fresh taste, a new story, in our stale world.

Congregations create seasoning pockets of grace in all kinds of ways. This happens, for example, when people who are homeless are included in worship and given an opportunity to contribute, or when those with mental illness or Alzheimer's are honoured, and supports are provided, so that they can participate meaningfully. This also occurs when children are given space to be loud and to ask questions and to share their thoughts and prayers. When a church is being faithful like this, it offers one of the only communities I can think of, in which each person is valued and included without belonging being contingent upon bank balance, education level, abilities, sporting prowess, postcode, visa status, colour, gender, occupation, culture or hairstyle.

I know, sadly, not all congregations offer this kind of unqualified hospitality. But this is the call of Jesus – to make room at the table for all. Like the ego-driven disciples, we need to get over our focus on power and status, and instead use our power for making space for everyone to be honoured and treasured, especially the marginalised. In doing so, we become a seasoning, healing presence, salted with fire.

Seasoning actions in a stale world

John Chrysostom had a reputation as an inspiring speaker and teacher. Indeed, Chrysostom was not John's surname, but rather an anglicised version of his nickname 'golden mouthed'. At times, people would break into applause after Chrysostom preached. His sermons were transcribed and distributed widely, even in his own lifetime, and his words continue to be poured over today.[13] Chrysostom was born in the mid 300s, in a period in which the Christian church and the Roman empire were becoming intwined in ways that were distorting Christianity. Chrysostom was a priest in Antioch and then, very reluctantly, was made Archbishop in Constantinople, current day Istanbul.

By all accounts, he was not seduced by the status of this role, or by the wealth and power that were flooding into the now legalised (and increasingly reputable and esteemed) church. Instead, as Archbishop, Chrysostom sought to bring the church's increasing excesses into line and organised for the opening of hospitals. In his preaching, Chrysostom raged against the hypocrisy of hoarding wealth and claiming to be a follower of Jesus. Chrysostom states:

> If you cannot remember everything, instead of everything, I beg you, remember this without fail, that to fail to share our own wealth with the poor is theft from the poor and deprivation of their means of life; we do not possess our wealth but theirs. (Chrysostom, *Homily 2, on the Parable of Lazarus and the Rich Man*)

---

[13] It must be acknowledged and lamented that Chrysostom speaks in woeful terms about Jewish people.

In graphic sharpness, Chrysostom underscores this point:

> Do you pay such honour to your excrements as to collect them into a silver chamber-pot when another person made in the image of God is perishing in the cold? (Chrysostom, *Homily 7 on the Letter to the Colossians*)

It may be unsurprising to hear that Chrysostom was not popular with the wealthy elite, or with those clergy who were relishing the increasing wealth and status accorded the church by the Roman empire. Chrysostom would still be unpopular today with those who proclaim prosperity theologies. He would also make for an uncomfortable guest preacher for those Christians hoarding wealth or contemplating major bathroom renovations.

Within Chrysostom's extensive preaching on Matthew's Gospel, he speaks of the importance of the church being salty. Chrysostom states:

> Why must you be salt? Jesus says in effect: 'You are accountable not only for your own life but also for that of the entire world. I am sending you not to one or two cities, nor to ten or twenty, not even to one nation, as I sent the prophets. Rather I am sending you to the entire earth, across the seas, to the whole world, to a world fallen into an evil state'. For by saying, 'You are the salt of the earth', Jesus signifies that all human nature has 'lost its taste', having become rotten through sin. For this reason, you see, he requires from his disciples those character traits that are most necessary and useful for the benefit of all. (Chrysostom, *Homily XV, Matthew 5:1, 2*)

For Chrysostom, Christians are called to be the seasoning salty presence in a world made stale by sin (by selfish ego-driven agendas and greed) and Christians do this by embodying Jesus' radical humility, generosity, mercy and non-retaliation. Chrysostom goes on:

> For first, the meek, and yielding, and merciful, and righteous, shuts not up their good deeds to themselves only, but also provides that these good fountains should run over for the benefit of others. And they again who are pure in heart, and peacemakers, and are persecuted for the truth's sake; they again order their way of life for the common good. "Think not then', he says, 'that you are drawn on to ordinary conflicts, or that for some small matters you are to give account'. 'You are the salt of the earth.' (Chrysostom, *Homily XV, Matthew 5:1, 2*)

To put this bluntly, for Chrysostom, being the salt that seasons in a world gone rotten, requires that Christians take Jesus at his word. I think this continues to be the call to the church.

The church loses its tastiness when it ignores the centrality of living like Jesus and as Jesus calls us to – in radical generosity and compassion – especially for those who are poor or who are marginalised. This is an essential call for the church not just because those in need should be supported. The church is also impoverished when it fails to heed Jesus' call, and instead becomes a self-serving, rather empty, social club. As Rev. Natalie Dixon-Monu reflects:

> When the church gave up its mission and its service and handed it over to the welfare state we lost our very life

blood. And why? Because there went God. A big chunk of God... There is something about missional acts that take us out. Unfortunately, we can get comfortable within our own communities, but it is when you step out of that into the world, with an intention of embodying God's presence and opening yourself up to the mutuality, there is a powerful feeding of the soul in that moment.

Across various congregations, dotted around the place in rural, regional and urban Australia, people are still getting on with this vital salty living and giving. Church run op-shops provide affordable clothing and save immeasurable tonnes of clothes from landfill. Not only this, church run op-shops often provide a space for friendly and respectful conversation and, in addition, link with other services, for example by providing clothing for asylum seekers or for people experiencing homelessness. Free English conversation classes, run by parishioners, offer support and friendship to new arrivals and refugees, people who often receive little government support. Craft groups provide integral links for people who are socially isolated. Soup kitchens and food programs provide the literal stuff of life, enough food to get through the week.

Accompanying this, and perhaps of equal importance, many food relief programs also provide cup of tea and kind conversation. Refugee welcome centres provide safe space and extensive supports for those who have had to flee everything. In the best of these diverse church offerings, people are always treated with dignity and honour. They are recognised as people who embody the presence of God, rather than seen as people of lesser importance, or as failures, or as problems to solve. Such expressions of being church also create authentic links between the 'serving' parts of the church and the worshipping community so that a dynamic, salty flow can exist between church members and participants as they enrich one another.

However, as Justin Martyr reminded us in the opening chapters of this book, living in salty mercy and generosity is not always tied up with being involved in church programs. This action-based salty kindness and compassion is also reflected in the countless ways individual Christians rally to care for others amidst the messiness and challenges of their own daily lives. This spicy, merciful living might be expressed in buying food for someone on the street and spending time in conversation together, making a meal for someone who is sick, living simply in order to be able to contribute large-scale tithing for those in need, or following up a person who is socially isolated or at a low ebb.

How sustaining might it be to imagine these (often unseen and unglamorous) daily compassionate choices as guerilla acts of salty seasoning in our world that so easily goes stale? Likewise, how powerful might it be to take seriously Jesus' parable in Matthew 25:31-46, that in living in radical compassion, it is here that we will encounter the divine? Rather than acting from any position of superiority, being salty, gracious people is about being ready for Christ to meet us in the eyes and words of others, especially those who are so often relegated to the 'no hopers' pile, by the 'powerful' in our often tasteless culture.

Combining words and deeds

If we hold together the ideas of salty seasoning words in Colossians *and* the embodied focus of being salty peace-making communities in the Gospel of Mark and in Chrysostom's writing, we are confronted with a powerful challenge. Here we discover that part of being a salty seasoning presence in the world, is being *gracious* advocates for mercy, justice, peace and the common good, in *both* words and actions. In becoming such advocates, we may draw out the flavours of compassion and care for all things.

We see glimpses of this kind of salty speaking and advocacy in Australia. On Palm Sunday, people from across various Christian denominations gather with hundreds and hundreds of others, to advocate for the rights of refugees and asylum seekers. Across church traditions, parishes advocate for greater care for the earth and action on climate change. They do this *because* of their Christian convictions about the earth's sacredness and the call for humans to care for all things. In the Synod of Victoria and Tasmania walking together as First and Second peoples is integral to our vision, and across the Uniting Church, at national and local levels, people continue to advocate for Indigenous rights, alongside, and learning from, the Uniting Aboriginal and Islander Christian Congress.

As individuals and as church communities, we are called into the sacred ordinary work (that is never complete) of speaking graciously and sparingly and acting with generosity and compassion, so that our world might be seasoned. This is a call into a gentle and radically different way of being. Jesus calls us to put down our power struggles, share our wealth and to become spicy pockets of kindness and generosity in which those considered the least are honoured and cared for. This call demands that we engage with the costly work of letting Spirit near us so that our ego-driven agendas can begin to be dismantled (see the contrasting lists of the works of the flesh and the fruit of the Spirit in Galatians for some clues about what this entails Galatians 5:16-26).

Through this process, we might actually be able to get over our selves enough to see that we are not the substance but the salt *and* be more able to recognise what God is already doing on the edges and to join in. When we do this, we might just draw out the good flavours of faith, hope and love in our global village that is often made bland by despair and the emptiness of self-seeking.

Wondering Questions

What is most challenging about the call in Colossians to season conversations by always speaking graciously?

Are you comfortable speaking about your faith in kind (little) ways? Why or why not?

Where do you see the church actually being a salty seasoner in the world by embodying Jesus' mercy, generosity and peace and advocating for justice and compassion?

Is your church community doing this? How might you lean into this call more?

Reflection and Prayer Resources

Light a candle.

Have some bread, olive oil and salt at the centre of your gathering.

Spend some time reflecting alone, or with your community, on the wondering questions.

Rest in some silence.

Close with the following prayer:

Jesus bread of life
to whom shall we go?
You have the words of eternal life.

In turn, take some bread, dip it in the oil and sprinkle a little salt on top and enjoy.

When everyone has eaten. continue the prayer:

May we be salty in our words,
may we be salty in our deeds,
drawing out the flavours of mercy and compassion
in your precious world
Amen.

Chapter Seven

Sweaty conclusions

Beyond idolatrous images of the church 'triumphant' and dismal mantras about church decline, there is a different story. The church is not dying – it is being refined. All the cultural accoutrements of church that have been welded onto our structures and have distorted our understandings of faithfulness are perishing. Thanks be to God. The church as the purveyor of respectability, the church as the hub of social activity, the church as the 'purity police', the church as the city fortress and ultimate authority – all of these forms of church are vanishing. In their wake, in this cultural moment, we are being given an extraordinary (and painful) opportunity to recognise what we had become and to change. As the lies of empire-shaped church are exposed for what they are, we can finally begin to do the hard work of becoming the church that Jesus calls us to be.

This book has chosen to focus on just one creative image that Jesus uses in the Gospels – the metaphor of being salt. If we take this imagery seriously and wrestle with it, our easy assumptions about being church are challenged. Beyond consumerist culture's lie that big is best and large numbers, or vast buildings, equate with success, within the metaphor of salt we discover the goodness of being little, like tiny grains.

In this metaphor, we are confronted with a different vision of faithfulness. Our purpose is not to maintain huge buildings or to offer shiny, on-trend programs that will gather in the crowds, instead our core purpose is to be spicy communities of grace. As Justin Martyr and the authors of *1 Clement* point to, at the heart of things, churches are called to be communities of love – who love the Holy One – Sacred Three, who experience the love of this God, who are changed by this love and who generously share this love with all.

In the imagery of salt, we are invited to carve out space for salty tears. As Paul indicates, if we are followers of Jesus, we are called to be communities of radical solidarity, weeping with those who weep and rejoicing with those who rejoice. In such communities of mutuality, we will no longer view one another as problems to solve. We will no longer be afraid of the place of weeping, doubt and sorrow because we will know that these are part of life for people of faith. When we lean into this way of being together, we defy our culture's destructive obsession with being happy, positive and *#living my best life*. By being communities in which lament and tears have a valued place, we carve out space for truth telling and, like the Psalmists before us, embody authenticity. In creating such spaces together, we also testify to the reality that the God of Jesus Christ weeps with us as we weep and can bring unexpected life in places of despair.

In the metaphor of salt, we re-discover the biblical imagery of good, dark, salty wombs. When the womb and birth imagery, found in Second Testament texts like John's Gospel and 1 Peter, are taken seriously, we discover female divine images – for it is she who rebirths us and nourishes us. In this womb imagery, we are also challenged to think in a different way about growth. Unlike consumerist culture's ideas of growth and productivity, womb growth is vulnerable, hidden, unpredictable and cannot be controlled. If we reclaim this biblical understanding of womb growth, we are challenged to put down our ego-driven agendas.

Womb-like growth comes with no guarantees, as so many women know. In taking this imagery seriously, the church is challenged to be fixated no longer on 'successful' outcomes. Instead, we are called to be open and alert to what God is already growing up within our midst and beyond our churches, especially on the edges, and to join in. Womb-like growth is an invitation into vulnerability – becoming reliant upon Christ's nourishment and Spirit's tender knitting together of the good new life in the middle of the messiness.

Within the imagery of salt, the church is also reminded of the core priority of preserving. However, this salty preservation work is not about propping up cultural habits or traditions. For Origen, this preserving work is essential for the whole world and is focused on the divine's embracing love for all things. To push this to a finer point, the core thing that we are called to preserve as Christians is the divine love disclosed in Jesus. We do this most authentically when we create spaces for people to be able to wrestle with the biblical text and theology and what this might mean for their lives.

There is more than this though. The way of Jesus is not simply a delicious, intellectual endeavour. We Christians make the astonishing proclamation that divine love gets *personal* in Jesus and that *each of us* is called into healing relationship with this Holy Human One. In the salty work of preserving the centrality of Jesus as a church, cultivating spaces to explore, question, experiment with and deepen practices of prayer that help us to *tune in* to the divine are integral.

Salt, thankfully, also draws out delicious tastes. To take this imagery seriously is to reconsider our place in the world. We are not the substance. Instead, if we understand ourselves as the salt that seasons, we have a different purpose all together. We are called to let the grace of God shake out of us wherever we go, so that the sweetness is drawn out for the benefit of all. As the author of Colossians reminds us, every conversation becomes a place for grace to be sprinkled.

However, like the seasoning of a meal, we need to recognise that a little goes along way. We are called to be prudent about how much we speak. In our own cultural context in the West, in which the church has done so much damage to people, this needs to be underscored. As Chrysostom proclaims, being a seasoning salty presence also challenges the church to cultivate actions based on Jesus' words and behaviour. Mercy, gentleness and generosity become the hallmarks of our collective and individual lives. In our compassionate and humble deeds, we season our global village that is so often made stale by selfishness and fear. In speaking and acting in mercy and peace, we are also called to advocate for justice and compassion, as we tell new stories about how our common life could be. Through embodying the kindness of Jesus, our salty presence as a church might – even yet – draw out the beautiful for us and for all things.

Sweaty conclusions

When Anne McCamish, an avid gardener and member at Richmond Uniting, heard about each of the chapters of the book, in a matter of fact voice she responded:

But you also sweat salt when you do hard work.

Anne is right. And this seems to me like a perfect place to end. We began in littleness and tears, we moved through the messiness and vulnerability of birth, we explored preserving and seasoning, let's end in sweat. It is good to end in sweat because if churches choose to engage seriously with the imagery of being salt, it will be hard work.

To move from the model of church as cultural edifice, proudly residing at the centre of society, right to the edges, will be costly. Putting down our culture's incessant lie that success equates with vastness is going to take the dismantling of many ego-driven agendas and it will hurt. Creating safe spaces for tears and lament will be unpopular. Cultivating space for womb-like growth, that is not focused on outcomes or our own efforts, will be vulnerable.

Preserving the centrality of Jesus and prioritising practices of prayer will be challenging, especially in those churches who have been told that if they make themselves more amenable to culture – and speak less about Jesus or religious experience – they will regain popularity or public credibility. And, perhaps most difficult of all, learning to shut up and to focus on the mundane, unfinished work of being excessively kind, is going to take a significant amount of metaphorical sweat. In some churches this will demand an internal cultural shift of epic proportions.

Let's not be afraid of the sweat. Most things of value take hard work. We need to let the sweat and the tears, the vulnerable growth and delicious tastes flow. In all of this hard work, I pray that we may begin to get free of the lies of empire and culture about what church is and instead become more like the church that Jesus speaks about – little pockets of saltiness.

Let us be messy, humble communities of compassion together – who try and fail and who forgive and try again. Let us know that we are not alone and that we are not called to do this being in our own strength (this is another empire lie). Instead, each step we take into being salty people, Jesus – the Word – the story of God in person – who could not be contained by all our violence, despair and death, is with us and will nurture us along the way.

Wondering Questions

What challenges you most in this book?

How might you live differently, as an individual or as a church, as you seek to be salty?

What would you like to learn more about?

Reflection and Prayer Resources

Light a candle.

Spend some time reflecting alone, or with your community, on the wondering questions.

Rest in some silence.

Pray (together) in your own words, about your desires for the church in your patch.

Sing or say the words of the hymn/song 'Lord Jesus, we belong to you' by Robin Mann and John Wilfred Kleinig (Together in Song, 686).

Close with the following prayer:

Ground of our being, Water of life, Fire of truth
Holy One – Sacred Three be with us as we go.
Please continue to cleanse us out
and spice us up for compassion –
as we journey with you on the pilgrim way.
Through Jesus we pray. Amen.